LUCKY TO BE HERE

Jack Bewes,
463 Lancaster Squadron

Compiled by Lyn McGettigan

Riverton
Press

LUCKY TO BE HERE
Jack Bewes,
463 Lancaster Squadron

ISBN: 978-0-6450335-1-9 (print)
ISBN: 978-0-6450335-2-6 (e-book)

Book design by Petr Kovarik

This book is copyright.
© Lyn McGettigan, 2023

Published by Riverton Press
www.rivertonpress.com

Riverton
Press

First published in 2023 by Riverton Press, Sydney, New South Wales, Australia.

CONTENTS

Dedication	1
Foreword	2
War Tonight	4
Jack's Memoir: "Lucky to be Here"	5
Fact – Not Romantic Trappings	18
What has changed?	20
Jack's Legacy	22
These Boys went to War	24
The Squadron & the Men	29
Hello England	34
Not All War	36
The Reality of War	44
Letters Written Between Airmen	65
The Propaganda Booklet	77
Training and War	80
Operations and Remarks	84
Flight Log Book	85
For All the Boys Who Did Not Return	90
Life After the War	92
Jack's Wife Pearl	96
Glossary	98
References	103
Our Memories	104
Acknowledgements	111

The Story of John Joseph (Jack) Bewes
1920-1999
Bomb Aimer, RAAF 423600
Lancasters
463 Squadron, Waddington, Lincolnshire

Compiled by Lyn McGettigan from Jack's Records:
Flying Log Book, Diary Recording all Sorties, Personal Diary,
Aircraft Mechanics Pocket Book, Handwritten Class Notes,
Letters between Airmen, Newspaper Articles, Photograph Albums.

DEDICATION

To the families of all airmen
whose fathers spoke little of the war
and left no records.

Thank you, Jack,
for all that you have left us,
for showing us the joy of living
and the satisfaction of achieving.

FOREWORD

This is the story of Jack Bewes and the men of his crew in 463 Squadron formed as part of RAF (Royal Air Force) 5 Group on 25 November 1943. The Squadron's motto, "Press on Regardless". was on their insignia – a star of seven points with four crossed sledge hammers. The Squadron flew Lancasters from Waddington, Lincolnshire, across Germany and France beginning the night after their formation with an attack on Berlin until the end of the War. Three of the Squadron's aircraft were especially modified and sometimes carried cameramen of the R.A.F. Film Unit. Each bombing raid and the results were filmed by the bomb aimer. The button used to drop the bombs activated the cameras to record the results.

463 Squadron flew 2,525 sorties in 180 bombing raids, of which Jack and Crew flew and survived 35. In these sorties 69 aircraft were lost in raids and a further 10 were destroyed in crashes. Jack's diaries are invaluable in that they describe his thoughts and those of the crew on their sorties and after they landed.

The Squadron suffered the highest percentage loss rate of Australian Squadrons. This, as well as the fact that the 463 was part of the 5 Group precision bombing group (of Dam Busters fame), could explain why Jack referred to 5 Group as "the Chop Squad".

Over 4,100 RAAF (Royal Australian Air Force) died. (W. Chorley. "RAF Bomber Losses in the Second World War").

Interlaced with all the facts is the part luck and "Johnnie's God" played in their sorties. It has been written that many crews had "good luck" charms. Jack and the crew had "Johnnie's God" and the Miraculous Medal of Mary.

The human side of war is revealed in his diaries, logbooks and letters. The coping mechanisms of humour, friendship, enjoyment of the present, looking forward to the future, are all too evident.

Waddington, May 1944

WAR TONIGHT

Target lit up ahead, 600 planes flying towards it. Night becomes day. Lights everywhere – clawing at the sky, flickering across the ground, fingers reaching for us. Red, green, yellow flares, red with green stars, green with red stars. Red and yellow ground markers. Red flare lighting target. Vivid white photo flare melds as the bomb aimer photographs his hit. A hot flat flare drifts down, hotter than the engine of the plane. The German missile hits that, not us. Candle flares in flat bomb cases open up, burn brightly and highlight the target. More flares indicate plane entry path to target. Flares indicate turning point for home. Smoke, haze obscuring. Smell of burning. Flak lights twinkle on the ground below as guns fire; searchlights rake the sky to cone our planes. A bright explosion. One of yours has copped it. The plane explodes in a blinding flash as the bombs and incendiaries go off. The burning funeral pyre plunges below. The city and the target burn.

Planes all around us. Duck and weave on your bombing run to avoid your own planes and the bombs dropping from them. Tapping on the fuselage. Ack ack bullets. Duck and weave. Enemy planes reflected in the clouds above, below and beside you, firing. Duck and weave.

Follow the exit flare. Run for home. Enemy aircraft firing and strafing. A wing and a prayer. Land safely.

Wait in hope for the others.

The Aeroplane, May 26, 1944   A clipping from Jack's papers.

"LUCKY TO BE HERE"
JACK'S MEMOIR

Written in the year before his death in 1999 (Unabridged)

Sydney prior to the War was like a big country town. Most people like myself went ballroom dancing during the week and on Saturday night. We played tennis Saturday and Sunday mornings and then went surfing on Sunday afternoon at Cronulla.

Hardly anyone drank as pubs closed at 6pm Monday to Saturday and closed all day Sunday. I never went to Bondi or Manly. Whilst overseas people asked, "What is Bondi like?" I went to Bondi when I came home.

Nobody would molest you at any time of the day or night regardless of where you were. My grandparents had a weekender at Woonona (near Wollongong) – the only house between the railway station and the beach. We used to spend the Christmas holiday there each year. We would never lock our house in Rockdale, all we did was close the front door. In 1938 my mate and I rode our pushbikes to Newcastle – up Good Friday, back Easter Sunday.

When war broke out I did not know which service to join permanently. As my uncle had served at Gallipoli and France during World War 1, I decided to wait for a call up to the militia and try it for three months. Militia personnel went in for three months and out for three months.

I was called up in early 1941 and served in an anti-aircraft battalion. Life was very boring – an odd aircraft. To defend the coast we camped at Miranda, slept in tents on the ground, no showers, shaves or change of clothes for ten days. Our camp was supposed to last for fourteen days. On the tenth a jeep arrived (jeeps were new in those days) and our colonel and adjutant went for a ride in it. It happened to be an enemy vehicle so the war was soon over. Back in camp at Ingleburn a night march was cancelled as it looked like rain and we might have got wet. Another day while exercising I was just about to fire the machine gun when the whistle sounded and we were told to pack up as it was time for lunch (what a Joke).

Soon after my first three months I received a call up for full time militia service plus a full time NCO's course. I rang them up and told them I would not be available as I was joining the Air Force. All the family thought I would be joining ground staff. I told them that the Air Force meant flying and were trained overseas both in Canada and the UK. This was a big plus as we had been very restricted in our movements prior to the war.

The medical examination took 1-1/2 days. Only 15 of the 30 odd people passed. I remember the last Doctor told me that I had some moles on my back and if shrapnel scraped my back I would bleed to death. I told him not to worry because if shrapnel came that close, I would die of fright.

Six months later we started training at Bradfield, Sydney. After three months we were told where we had come in class and asked what we wanted to be trained for. I told them I was happy to do any job provided I trained overseas. I was told I was the first one not to request to be trained as a pilot. I said I would love to be a pilot but I wanted to train overseas even as a gunner. The C O became cranky and said you will go overseas and train as a navigator and that I would be gone within two weeks. I was allowed to go home each night until 10pm. I told mum and the family that the night I did not come home it meant that I was gone. We left Sydney at 6pm, glad I did not contact the family who would have come as all the mothers were crying etc. We travelled to Albury and changed trains. In those days each state had a different rail gauge i.e. some rail tracks were wider.

When we arrived in Melbourne we boarded a ship for the trip across Bass Strait to Launceston in Tasmania then by train to Hobart. Ninety percent of us were seasick on the boat. We had two days in Hobart and then boarded the "Ile De France" en route to Canada. On board were mostly German POW's bound for Canada. All spoke excellent English – most had been educated at Eton or Oxford. I was placed in charge of the food tables so I had a lot to do with them. As they were only allowed one cigarette a day I used to give them a few. However the C O found out and said that unless it stopped he would court martial the person responsible. I never gave any more to them but somehow or other I happened to lose the odd packet. One of them gave me a beautiful silver ring with an eagle and swastika on it. I wore it during the war. People would look at it and then at me. I would tell them that I had a German cousin and that if I was shot down to show the ring and ask for him.

One day on the boat we were told there was a shortage of bomb aimers (a new category as previously the navigators did both jobs). I asked what it entailed – it meant you learnt to fly, navigate, operate wireless and gunnery and replace anyone who was killed.

At that time most bomb aimers were scrubbed pilots. I volunteered mainly because the course was shorter – five months compared to eight months. I would see more of what was going on (navigators never moved out of their cabins) and also, I would get to England much quicker.

We landed in San Francisco and went by train to Vancouver (Canada). On the way up there was a snowfall and as none of us had ever seen snow, we jumped out while the train was held up and had snow fights. We had to laugh when the locals said it was amazing how we learnt to speak English on the boat coming over. Their idea then, and possibly now, is that the only language spoken was Aborigine.

We trained at Edmonton (Canada) and Lethbridge (England). On my first flight the pilot thought I was a scrubbed pilot and asked me if I would fly it while he went to the toilet. When he got down the back of the aircraft the others asked him who was flying. He said the bomb aimer who was a scrubbed pilot. After being told that it was the first time I had been in an aircraft he soon rushed back.

Christmas 1942 was spent at Spokane in the USA. Whilst at Midnight Mass I was asked what I was doing Christmas Day and if possible, they would like me and a couple of my mates to have lunch with them. This we did and it was beautiful – we even sliced our own meat. Whilst in Canada we used to go ice skating. As we were not able to skate the local girls helped us.

When we graduated we were interviewed by the C O. The first ten in the class were to receive a commission and the rest non-commission i.e. sergeants. I finished in the first five. When I was interviewed the first question was "What does your father do?" When I said that he had died before I went to High School the interview was over. Talk about class distinction. One chap who finished outside of the first 10 was granted a commission when he informed them that his father was general manager for Metro Goldwyn Mayer Film Studios.

Before we proceeded to England we had 10 days off and went to Niagara Falls and New York. When we went to Radio City to see the Rockettes, instead of walking up to the first floor we went by lift. No theatre in Sydney had a lift in those days. We also went and had a drink at Jack Dempsey's Bar and we went to the top of the Empire State Building. The fast lift went up the first 80 floors non-stop. The top floors were not occupied as the building swayed in the breeze. Cars below looked like matchboxes.

Nothing happened on the boat from Halifax (Canada) to Liverpool (England). We went by train from Liverpool to Brighton south of London. There was only the Channel between us and France. We passed through London and all of us kept awake so we could see the city. Nothing, as there was a blackout each night.

From Brighton all the various categories were sent to #27 Operational Training Unit at Lichfield, just out of Birmingham, so that they could meet and form crews. The pilot and the two gunners came from Perth whilst the navigator, wireless operator and myself came from Sydney. We spent time here getting to know each other and started flying in Wellingtons (2-engine aircraft). We went from there to an Advanced Flying Unit at Winthorpe and then to a Conversion Unit at Newark where we changed from two to four engine aircraft i.e. Lancaster. It was here that our crew was increased from six to seven with the addition of a Flight Engineer, Sandy, from Scotland. And here I met a WAAF (Doreen) whose parents asked myself and two others to spend Xmas with them. Gee it was terrific. It was then I found out that Doreen was married, as I addressed her mother as Mrs. Allan, to be told she was Mrs. Field and that

Doreen was married. Her husband was in the Middle East. We remained very good friends for the whole time I was in England.

Prior to Xmas 1943 we had been transferred to 463 Squadron at Waddington, just out of Lincoln. On New Year's Eve we went into Lincoln but Maurie (Wireless Op) and Bill (mid-upper gunner) stayed in camp. They were briefed to fly with another crew who were two short. We found out next morning when we did not see them, that they had been shot down and the whole crew killed. It made you realise just how short life can be for Air Crew.

We got two replacements and started flying in mid-January with a trip to Berlin. Prior to going to the Squadron, we had done a trip to Paris dropping leaflets and getting some experience. Only two crews went and I saw my best mate's crew shot down over Paris.

Eric was picked up by the French who asked him his age. When he said 20, he was told that he was too young to be placed with the girls so he went with the boys. He finally walked over the Pyrenees. He joined another crew and he was shot down and killed a week before we were due to meet.

The night following our Berlin trip we bombed Magdeburg. We used to carry one 4,000 lb bomb plus ten or more of 1,000 lbs. After our second trip I rang Mr. and Mrs. Field and told them I was OK. A few days later I was called in to the Squadron leader's office (W/C Kingsford-Smith). He asked me to listen to a tape and tell him who was speaking, it turned out to be me. The military police had listened to my conversation with the Fields, they wanted me court-martialled. The C O said he would think about it but in the meantime to continue flying. On the next six trips I felt like bailing out as the threat of a court martial hung over my head. Finally I was told that the matter was closed.

At 10 am we would know if there was war that night, whether you were scheduled to fly or if there would be no war. You had a break each month. Also there was no flying during the full moon period. We had 24-hour leave passes unless you were required to fly.

If not required to fly, one would leave camp immediately, reason being that if a crew was short and you were around, they would get you to fill the vacancy. Life was short enough with your own crew, let alone fly with others.

I remember one day when I had to brief four crews on what to expect. I told them not to take anything for granted and to double check. On their first trip three of the four crews failed to return. The remaining crew asked me what might happen. I told them not to worry as only 50% were killed. They were killed on their second operation.

Everybody helped everybody especially if you were hit. We had to help our mid-upper gunner into his turret before take-off. He often said to me, "Johnny, if we get hit will you come back and help me get out of this turret?" My reply was, "Harold, if anything happens to you and you feel cold air around your legs, you will know I have bailed out." Actually, if anything had happened, I and the others would have helped him. The pilot was the only one who held a parachute, the rest of us just placed them in the aircraft near you.

I recall one rear gunner whose plane was hit and his turret jammed so that he could not get his parachute. Rather than burn to death he opened his doors and fell out backwards at 23,000 ft. He was not meant to die as he hit a tree and landed in a snow drift. All he suffered was a broken leg.

The constant flights (approx. 7-8 hours) proved too much for some crew. Their nerves would go and they just could not fly. Instead of being taken off flying and sent to ground duties minus rank and aircrew badge, they would have their rank and air crew badge ripped off and moved to a station in their original uniform and cleaned out latrines etc. Their papers and discharge papers were stamped LMF (lack of moral fibre) i.e. a coward.

One pilot on our squadron had something go wrong each trip e.g., motor cut. He never crossed the French Coast on his first 17 trips. On his 18th trip he crossed the coast but never returned (he was a typical nerve case).

The German fighter pilots were totally dedicated. Over the target they would fly through their own anti-aircraft gun fire to get at you. Besides that, they would send up scarecrows that looked like aircraft exploding. It was good to leave the target but even so, you could not relax even after you crossed the

English Coast. The odd German fighter would also cross the coast and put their navigation lights on and attack you, just as you were going in to land. After we finished our tour of operations we were posted to various operational training units to train new recruits. This is what happened to Sandy, our Flight Engineer, who was with this new recruit team when they were shot down and all killed just as they were landing.

After snow had fallen, some German planes would be painted white with cannons pointing upwards. They would fly underneath you and then fire. As you can see, one cannot relax for a moment from the time you took off to the time you landed. Mostly we would arrive back between 2am to 3am and then play snooker or billiards until the tension eased in one to two hours.

About 600-700 aircraft flew on each operation and bombed within twenty to thirty minutes. They flew from about 17,000 to 23,000 feet, so there were certainly a few aircraft about. It is a wonder more did not collide.

I remember one night I looked up and there was this bomber above us with bomb doors open. I yelled to the pilot to dive port. This he did and the bombs fell beside us. If I had not looked up, we would have copped the lot.

It was important you flew within the group. You could smell the chloride. New crews dropped "nickel" (silver strips) which blurred the radar screens. One night we wandered out of the group. The Germans lined us up as regards height, speed etc. Unfortunately for them, good for us, they fired their anti-aircraft guns too early. All the shells exploded in front of us.

Our guns only had a range of approx. 800 yards. The Germans knew this so one fighter would put his navigation lights on and fly about 1000 yards from you. His mate just waited until you fired and then he blasted you with cannon shells. This happened to us. Col said he would turn towards the decoy and for me to fire. I said, "No". Thank God I did as the other plane would have blasted us.

Another danger was that, depending on height and weather conditions, the engines would leave contrails i.e. white smoke lines. The German fighters would follow them and then blast you with cannons. To lose contrails you had to change height etc.

The worst trip was to Nuremburg. Somehow the Germans found out our course, height etc and were waiting for us. Col asked me to watch for the markers. I said, "the marker is straight ahead". Then I saw about six other markers which were actually our planes being shot down. Suddenly a blast of cannon fire from a fighter and the plane ahead of us just blew up. Then more went the same way. Col said, "Man the front guns", which I had to do standing up. I said I could not do so as, boy, were my legs shaking. Len (Rear Gunner) said, "Johnnie, what is happening?" I said, "Don't worry. You will see it all if and when we get through". Planes kept exploding and being coned by searchlights. This was the worst trip of the war: 170 planes shot down or crashed over France and England out of a total of approximately 750. Another night like that and we would not have enough planes to continue the missions. About 800 aircrew were killed.

The Pathfinder Squadron had the worst job. They used to take off 20-30 minutes earlier than us. They would drop markers every so often so as to keep us on course. Over the target they would drop markers to show us where to bomb, also sky markers if there was cloud over the target.

Life was even shorter for them than for other aircrew. At first the (Pathfinder) Squadron comprised volunteers but in the end each Squadron nominated a different crew for each month, i.e. if a crew was required you would just go whether you liked it or not.

On another trip we lost a motor. Rather than turn back (the trip would not have been counted) I said, "We will drop a couple of bombs". I noticed a German farmhouse all lit up. I did not aim at the house but the bombs fell about 300 yards from it. Boy, did the lights go out fast.

While life was not good, there were funny times. One night Col asked Peter (Navigator):

"How far to the Coast?"

Peter said, "35 or 25 minutes".

Col got annoyed and said, "Why did you not give the correct figure the first time?"

Pete said, "Col, we have just run into a hundred mile per hour head wind. By the way, would you like me to step out and push the bastard?"

End of conversation.

All aircrew were obliged to complete 30 ops (if they survived), have six months off and then do a further 20 trips with a different crew. If they so desired, they could do 45 straight ops and then not be required to fly again unless they volunteered. Very few crews got to 10, let alone 30.

As we had worked well as a crew, we decided to do 45. Our first four trips were OK but on the fifth trip (number 35 in all), we were supposed to fly at 17,500 feet and a course of 240 on our second leg.

When we turned into the second leg the Germans put up a box barrage between 17-18,000 feet.

I asked Col was he going above it.

Col said, "No. We are flying at 17,500". I then asked him to go around it but again he said, "No, as we were to fly on a course of 240". We flew straight into the middle of the barrage and boy, did we cop it. Flak hit the windscreen and Sandy thought he had lost his head. I said,

"You must have it as I have never heard of anyone talking through his neck.".

When we finally landed we told Col to tell the C O we were not flying anymore. He tried to convince us to go on, but nobody said anything. As far as we were concerned Col had had it.

I would like to say that aircrew, if not flying, certainly enjoyed themselves. We were well paid – 25 shillings per day plus flying pay. Average wages those days were about 80 shillings per week. We were welcomed at each pub. While England may have had limited food, there was ample beer and cigarettes. The older people used to challenge us to a game of darts for a pint of beer. One night Len and I won and they did not have the money to buy, so we said it should be the best of three games and they won the next two. We just could not hit the board.

Air Crew were certainly well fed: baked dinners or bacon and eggs. Bacon and eggs were mainly what you received when you got back. They certainly saved on eggs as a lot did not come back.

When I had leave I used to spend it with Mr. and Mrs. Field. I used to take them out for a drink etc., even mow their lawns. The two girls at home were Sheila 16 and Mavis 13. Sheila and I would go to the local dance. We won the slow Foxtrot one night and received a bag of apples. When I had a night off I would go over to Newmark by train (30 miles) and have a drink with Doreen. Her mum and dad knew of this. Her mum said, "It's good you meet her. We know she's in safe hands". As I said before, we were just good friends.

One night whilst in London I went to Wembley. The dogs were running so I put five pounds on the favourite. It led all the way until, when 100 yards from home, it decided to go to the toilet and finished last. You can see why I do not bet these days.

When in London you slept in a big dormitory. You had to put your clothes under the mattress otherwise they would be gone by morning. One night I could not get a bed so I went to the local police station and asked if they had an empty cell. It was one of my best night's sleep.

One night Len and I bumped into two street girls. After being advised it was five pounds, or 30 shillings around the corner standing up, I said we would rather go and sit in a pub and drink beer. Anyhow, it was not worth the risk. Too many caught the disease and as there was no cure, they just killed themselves over Germany. Still, it was an experience and that was why we went overseas – to gain experience and meet all types.

I went back to 27 0TU at Lichfield to do my six months. Whilst I was on operations I received a Commission. The first night I was in charge of the Sergeants' mess. All complained about the food. I told them that I had eaten it the night before and had no problems. At 10pm I went to close the bar. I finished closing it at midnight as they all kept buying me drinks.

Even though it was wartime, all officers had a Batman who tidied your room. At Lichfield, the Batman was a woman. She had been a street girl in London. Instead of waking you up, she would ask you to move over. She was soon discharged.

When that was over I was sent by mistake to the centre where the newly finished aircrew were sent prior to their six month's break. They told me they did not know what to do in my case and to come back in two days. When I returned they said they had some bad news, I would be going back to Australia. I went to Brighton on the train and from there to Liverpool to catch our boat. We were held up for 30 minutes in London (signal failure). Rockets were landing all over London. I thought, "Just my luck for a rocket to fall on the train".

We came home via the Bay of Biscay (off Spain) and the Panama Canal. We first docked before we went through the Canal. It was here we saw a chap carrying a stalk of bananas. The English chaps had never seen a banana. Next thing, all that was left was the stalk. We saw Sydney Heads at approximately 3pm. We came into the Harbour and anchored off Mosman. We docked next morning at about 6am and were taken by bus to Bradfield Park. The first person I met was a WAAF (Joan Hobson) with whom I used to work. I knew then I was home. Next Mum arrived and we went home to a "Welcome Home" party. I remember Grandma said to me, "My son went to war (1914-1918) and came home OK, now my grandson has been to the War and come home. I can now die in peace". She died in 1947. Some people were envious of where I had been. They said, "What a good holiday". I told them they could have come if they had signed up.

I realise now that I was not 100% after I came home. It took me a few years to come back to normal. I even left a good job and transferred to a country job. It was the best thing I did as by the time I finally came back to Sydney (children were all starting High School – they got a better education and better jobs), I was back to normal.

After I arrived back, I was given five week's leave. As they had no four engine bombers i.e. Lancasters, I was one of six people sent to Melbourne for six weeks to do an Air Observers Course. I stayed with one of my mates,

Alan Withers. I went to football each Saturday. Cigarettes were very difficult to get. One day I gave a lady on a tram a packet (she asked if she could have one). We both got off at the one stop. She asked me to drop in for a drink. I said, "No thanks". She said, "Don't worry. My husband is doing 12 months in Albury jail".

After Melbourne I was sent to Tamworth (supplied with a car) to observe all aircraft in the district. The various posts would phone in. In October the Air Force boys asked me to a night out at Attunga. Whilst having a drink I noticed this nurse sitting with a group of other nurses. She was most attractive. I asked her to come over to the bar, which she did, and we started going out together. We became engaged in January 1946 and married at the end of March 1946. We have been married over 50 years and have enjoyed our lives together – dancing, tennis, golf etc. My wife's maiden name was Pearl Rose. What a pearl she has been to me and many others.

I have only been in one Anzac Day march in Sydney. There are only two left of the people I trained with, flew with and socialised with. I therefore am happier to go to Church on Anzac Day and say a few prayers for the ones who did not come back. The crew used to make me go to Church every Sunday, snow or rain (whether we flew Saturday or not) while they slept in as they reckoned my God looked after us. They did not have to do it as I would have gone anyway.

The following poem gave some idea of the life of aircrew.

And he's bending o'er the bombsight with the tracer flying by,

Luftwaffe above, flak guns behind, explosions fill the sky.

And he knows the trip's half over but he knows the worst's to come,

When they turn for home the route is known and yet they're forced to run,

And when they make it back and safely landed on the ground

The waiting for the "tailenders", the aircrew milling round. OK!

The waiting and the watching, quiet talking in the Mess.

The percentages were frightening, each day meant less and less

Of the mates, those dear old diggers with common love of home.

Aged nineteen years! What school was this?

And each man thinks alone.

Sydney Morning Herald. January 1948. Pg 10.
(Poet and title unknown)
Memoir Written 1998 (Jack died 1999)

FACT – NOT ROMANTIC TRAPPINGS

This newspaper letter, found amongst Jack's clippings, tells the story of why so many men went to war. It tells the story, factually, not romantically, and not as History likes to paint it.

There seems to be a common impression that the chief reasons for enlisting in WW2 were patriotism, hatred of the enemy, fear of invasion, etc. but during my service in the RAAF from 1940-1946 I can't remember any such sentiments expressed by fellow servicemen.

Not that we were concerned with heroics. Things like that just happened.

First it was just a game, a chance to share the public adulation for men in uniform, but when the novelty wore off, life in the services, except when one's life was directly threatened, was just another job.

No doubt some forfeited career opportunities by joining up, but don't forget that the Depression and a high rate of unemployment, especially in country areas, was still with us in 1939.

As a young man growing up in a depressed country area, I, and many like me, had no feelings of hate towards Adolf Hitler. Far from loathing him, many of us were grateful to him for rescuing us from a slow death through unemployment and boredom.

Newspaper clipping, written by J. Andersen of Campsie.
(Source and date unknown)

WHAT HAS CHANGED?

This clipping (edited) paints the cold hard results of war and recognition of the damaged men who returned. What is pertinent in this article is sadly relevant today.

"RAAF Memorial Asks for Money to Treat the War Neurotics.

Yesterday we launched a competition to raise funds for the RAAF Memorial Centre appeal.

The object of the appeal is to:

*Build a Memorial Club for ex-servicemen and women in honour of those who died in the Second World War.

*Build readjustment centres for the treatment of ex-service men and women in civil life.

*Continue the rehabilitation of men and women in civil life.

*Find permanent jobs for discharged men.

Especially should they be anxious to support the Memorial committee's proposal to spend money on readjustment centres for treating neurotic ex-servicemen.

This is a job the Government has shamefully neglected.

It has failed to recognise that the mental casualty of war is not a lunatic to be herded in the ordinary asylum.

His is a form of sickness we can cure if we go about the job in the right way. Otherwise we condemn the sufferer to a life of deepening misery.

The Memorial Committee's plan is to imitate what has been done in Canada, which has built a series of rehabilitation farms throughout the Dominion where the war neurotic, under expert guidance, can find his way back to reality and society in agreeable surroundings.

The RAAF did a magnificent job for Australia and for Britain during the war.

These are the boys who took the Lancasters over Germany, led dog fights over the Channel, blasted the Japs up and down the coast of New Guinea.

They were the most gallant of all the services, which is saying a lot.

War is a ghastly affair for all, but for the aircrew it is just a little more ghastly. The strain of the combat left severe wounds on the minds and spirits even of those who came out without a physical scratch.

Now the RAAF Memorial Committee offers the people of this City an opportunity to put in concrete form some of the admiration we so freely expressed during the war.

Let us prove that we are not content to give cheap words only".

Daily Telegraph, January 9, 1947

JACK'S LEGACY

We knew that Jack had kept diaries, clippings and photos from the war. I don't even think we were aware that he had kept them in the trunk that had been with him since the day he enlisted. He kept this under the house possibly because he didn't particularly want the reminder of his war years closer, or possibly because it was a big old tin trunk and houses in those days weren't big enough to store too much in, or simply because mum didn't want the house cluttered up.

When Jack died, we looked through it. The trunk was brown, rusty and battered, with handles on each end. On the front panel, roughly scratched in bold letters:

F/O BEWES A423600 RAAF

Inside was a personal treasure trove – diaries of wartime sorties, diaries of his personal life off the base, of the people he met, the experiences of Jack and his mates. There were training log books from Canada and England and a propaganda leaflet that was dropped over Germany. There were newspaper clippings of the boys coming home, articles written about how the war had affected them, poems and cartoons. A treasure trove written by those who actually were there showing their resilience and courage.

Why didn't we ask him about his war experiences? Perhaps as children he was just our dad and we were used to him as a constant, kind father. Perhaps he didn't want to talk about them. Whatever the answer, they are recorded now.

Jack wrote his memoir just before he died. This memoir provided a guideline to amalgamating the diaries, photographs and memorabilia to provide a rare insight into what war was really like. Together they humanise the cold hard facts of textbooks, the deaths of so many and the coping mechanisms these boys used. "Boys" is not a term used lightly – damaged men is what these experiences turned them into. Listening to these voices so baldly stating facts, downplaying grief and recording moments of humour while bombs were falling around them, is a humbling experience.

There is no diary of how Jack coped when he returned. All he records in his memoirs is "I realize now that I was not 100% when I came home". We didn't realise it. But a worry my mother must have had for many years constantly keeps returning to memory – "I hope Jack is alright". We heard this one Friday night when dad was due home from Sydney, Dad had travelled to Sydney from Baradine by train to complete a "Personnel Officers' Course" (probably called H R today as it involved solving personal as well as work-related problems).

He returned to continue the life he left behind, married now with a wife and family, coping with his humour and by throwing himself once again into a social life. There was no need for a diary now. Life was being lived.
As children we heard the names of his wartime friends. These diaries "flesh out" for us Doreen and her family, Col, who had settled back in Perth, and Jack Spratt, in Nambucca Heads, all of whom he kept in touch with until he died. There was a bond there that we or their partners would never feel and that words could never express.

Planes in snow, 463 Squadron

THESE BOYS WENT TO WAR

They took their humour with them. They needed it.

Jack's life was typical of the boys who set off on their great adventure. One of five children, he was born on 28 October 1920 at Rockdale, Sydney. His parents were Maud Coombes and John Joseph Bewes. He was a talented tennis player who played Saturday and Sunday at Rockdale Lawn Tennis Association. On Sunday afternoons he surfed at Cronulla. On Saturday night he taught and danced at Petersham Town Hall. He holidayed at his grandparents' home in Balranald when young, and then at their weekender at Woonona. Pushbikes were a common form of transport then and he and his mate would ride from Rockdale to Newcastle on long weekends.

He was educated at St Joseph's Convent Rockdale till the end of 1932. He then obtained a scholarship to De La Salle College Ashfield. He left there at the end of 1936 after passing the Intermediate Certificate. Jack lost his father at the age of 12. Although he won the scholarship to De la Salle Ashfield, he left at age 15 to help support the family. After passing the Public Service Examination he took a position as a Junior Clerk in N.S.W. State Public Service.

Jack was 21 when he set out for War and it is not common at that age to dwell on the dark side of life. This is the age of invincibility. The sense of adventure, the typical young man's pranks and joie de vie continued throughout their training. Jack decided to try the Army as his Uncle Fred had served at Gallipoli. Jack forgot that Fred had suffered severely from the effects of Mustard Gas. However, his career was not to be in the army. He was stationed at Miranda, Sydney, and remembers that a night march was cancelled because it was about to rain. That, and the fact that the army considered lunch was more important than training, decided him to enlist in the Air Force. More the go really – adventure overseas. He enlisted on 25 November 1941. First Canada for training, then Britain for the "real stuff" of which, as yet, they had no real concept.

As part of the British Commonwealth Training Scheme, they set off on the journey to war. This scheme, the Empire Training Scheme (as it was called in Australia), was to train aircrew for eventual transfer to the Royal Air Force to defend Britain (officially beginning on 29 April, 1940). His first encounter, after a training stint in Hobart, was with German Prisoners of War who had been interned on Bruny Island. The Australians and the Germans were en route to Canada aboard the Île de France. The British Government had asked Canada that their German war prisoners be interned there so I can only assume that as we were part of the Empire, the same applied to the Prisoners of War in Australia. The Australian boys on that ship found that many of the German prisoners were the same age as them. It must have been hard then and later on, as these men had seen the human side of war before any battle. The humanising of the enemy then had its effect, as Jack often said that he realised they were bombing civilians inadvertently and this is illustrated in his memoirs when he describes the release of bombs (all bombs had to be dropped before returning to base) near a German farmhouse that was ablaze with lights.

"I didn't want to kill the family," he said, "Just warn them."

The lights went off.

The trip over must have been exciting for these young men. It was the first time on a ship for many and the route was a voyage of discovery. On the way over they stopped at Auckland and had time there for sightseeing. They arrived in Pearl Harbour on 18 November 1942 and it appears, from photographs where they crowded onto every vantage point on the boat, that their sightseeing there was only around the Harbour itself. Then on to San Francisco on 24 November 1942. Again, from photographs, they crowded on deck to see the Golden Gate Bridge and Alcatraz. Then they were bundled into trains on their way to Edmonton.

Out comes the boyish side. Most of the boys had never seen snow. When the trains stopped at Eugene they piled out to feel the snow and have snow fights, just like any kids in a white wonderland. They wore no hats, no gloves, no coats. They photographed the group and the fun, no doubt to send home.

First sight of snow.   Eugene, Oregon, USA, 25 November 1942

They went sight-seeing in Vancouver, this time wearing coats, and laughing as seagulls dive-bombed them. They must have gotten over the novelty of the snow by then. By the time they had reached Blue River in the Rockies, they declared that they were world travellers. In Jasper they played in the snow with local children – these boys who were not much past boyhood themselves.

When they arrived at Lethbridge, Alberta, Canada, in December 1942, they were kitted out, and there are photographs of them posing in this "paraphernalia" – helmet, goggles, padded suits complete with whistle blower and miniature compass sewn somewhere in the suit, gloves, dark brown rubber galosh boots lined with sheepskin and zipped at the front. What feelings would have gone through their minds – pride? trepidation? All feelings still overlaid with a sense of adventure? They were training, reality had probably not set in, but then the human mind would have probably pushed any sense of what they were facing deep into its recesses.

Jack was a bomb aimer. At Edmonton (Canada), Lethbridge (Canada) and West Freugh (Scotland), he was trained in map reading, navigation, gunnery, bombing, photography and as a pilot. The Bomb Aimer appeared to be the "jack of all trades" on a Lancaster. He was trained to take over all crew positions if necessary. Training at West Freugh was on Anson and Botha aircraft. The Botha used there as a training aircraft in 1943 is worth mentioning and it is doubtful if the airmen trainees were told anything about the plane. It had been acquired by the RAF in December 1938. It was a 4-seater reconnaissance plane and a torpedo bomber which saw little action. It was under powered, was unstable, and the views to rear and side were virtually non-existent – useless for reconnaissance. Worse, it was sent to training units that had Anson aircraft. From Jack's diary it appears that it was used when crews were practising gunnery and it is lucky that his time in it was short – one and a half hours. The Botha was retired from all service in September 1944.

Edmonton provided a bit of light relief with its ice-skating rink. If the boys had had fun throwing snowballs in Jasper they must have laughed as many of them lurched and fell on the skating rink outside the base hangers, often with the local girls trying to teach them. Fun for all.

It was in Edmonton that Jack was recruited by the crew as their direct link to a God or a Power that many couldn't identify. A bicycle was bought for Jack and so began a routine that would continue all their flying years. Jack was regularly sent to Sunday Mass – rain, hail or snow. It was often rain and snow. This bicycle was loaded onto the ship with them and Jack's Sunday Masses continued in England. The crew may have slept in on Sundays, even after a Saturday sortie, but Jack could not. "They did not have to do it (make me go), as I would have gone anyway". The men had a belief and a respect for "Johnnie's God". They graduated from Edmonton on 1 April 1943.

Towards the end of July, the crew were given ten day's leave before leaving Halifax for England and the War. They went from Toronto to Niagara

Falls. The trains and the standard of service they experienced on the trip would have been something new for most of the boys. They were seated at white linen covered tables with appropriate glassware and flatware. It must have been cold. In outside photographs they were now all wearing their overcoats.

From Niagara to New York, where they must have been acclimatised to the snow, or it was youth where cold is not felt, or was the weather warmer? There are many photos of them in their Dress Blues (Blue battledress blouse and trousers and black tie), cigarettes sometimes in mouths if it was a larrikin-type photo. New York would have been breathtaking and awesome. They saw the Rockefeller Centre, 5th Avenue, the Empire State Building and Central Park – the stuff of the American movies so popular in picture shows back home in Australia. Sydney would have been lucky to have had many buildings over three stories then and very little traffic. But the experience that would have been the lasting memory was "The Stage Door Canteen".

This had opened in New York in March 1942 in the basement of the 44th Street Theatre and could hold 500 people at each of the four shifts per night. Food was provided – sandwiches, cakes, doughnuts – and served by Hollywood actors and comedians – Bette Davis, Lauren Bacall, Marlene Dietrich, Gertrude Lawrence, Red Skelton, Bing Crosby, Walter Pidgeon. The Canteen was open to enlisted men and non-commissioned officers, black or white. No alcohol was allowed – milk, fruit juice and cider were served instead.

Jack remembered this well, especially the dances he had with many of the celebrity hostesses to the music of the Big Bands – Benny Goodman, Glenn Miller, Tommy Dorsey. He told me he had no lack of partners. He was a very good dancer. It must have been good – there was no mention of lack of alcohol or the substitute soft drink. From what Jack told me verbally, there was a limit on the time you could stay – two hours – before the next group came in.

What a farewell before the realities of war became their life!

THE SQUADRON & THE MEN

Jack and the crew flew in a Lancaster. The 463 was an Australian Squadron formed (from C Flight of 467 Squadron) as part of 5 Group on 25 November 1943 at Waddington, Lincolnshire and was first commanded by Wing Commander Rollo Kingsford-Smith (nephew of Sir Charles Kingsford-Smith). The Squadron's last mission was 25 April 1945. Jack's crew were Australian with the exception of a Scotsman, Sandy.

The 463 Squadron flew 2,525 sorties, lost 69 aircraft in battle and 10 in crashes in its 17 months of operation. It was sad to note that a crash over the base in Waddington was flown by a pilot on his first sortie. Of the 546 casualties lost by this squadron, 226 were Australian. This was the highest loss rate of any Australian Squadron. Each Lancaster had a crew of seven. The 463, with the highest casualties, lost 226 airmen, the crew of 78 aircraft. The life expectancy of a Bomber crew was 13 missions. Jack and his crew flew 35 sorties from 20/1/44 – 27/6/44. His God truly looked after him. An interesting fact involved the Miraculous Medal of Mary that Jack and the crew hung in the cabin of their Lancaster. While many crews had "good luck charms", I would like to think that their medal meant more to them than a good luck charm. The next crew that flew that plane threw the medal out before they flew their first sortie. They did not return.

The Avro Lancaster was a true bombing machine. Bombs of various sizes, depending on the mission, could be loaded as well as incendiaries under its 33-foot-long fuselage. It had a wingspan of 102 feet with four engines. The wingspan dwarfed the fuselage of the plane but gave it awesome lifting power. It was black as it was to be a war time night bomber. It cruised at 293 miles per hour (275 mph with a full load) and carried 1,077 gallons of gasoline in each wing. Its range of 2,700 and 3,000 miles meant that it had the range to bomb far into Germany and return. It could cruise at altitudes above 20,000 feet. In spite of its size and load it was highly manoeuvrable, able to duck and dive to avoid flak and German fighters.

Although a formidable fighting machine, the Avro Lancaster had drawbacks and these contributed to the loss of airmen. The aircraft carried a very heavy bombing load and the location of the escape hatches was poor. The Lancaster was hard to escape from in the event of being hit or in a crash. If shot down it was estimated that only 15% of men would survive. In spite of this the Lancaster was not modified because modification would take too long and as many planes as possible were needed for the war effort.

Jack was a Bomb Aimer on a Lancaster of 463 Squadron. The bomb aimer's compartment was the Perspex nose situated in the front of the aircraft at a level below that of the main cockpit. Lying on his stomach, he needed to remain calm in spite of the searchlight and flak he could see coming up at him and the plane. Looking through the bombsight in the large Perspex blister, the Bomb Aimer would guide the aircraft over the target and, when it came into the bombsight, release the bomb load. From his position in the plane, he could assist both the pilot and the navigator with map reading and identification of approaching targets, as well as over the target, as is evidenced from entries in his diary.

As well, the Bomb Aimer was responsible for operating the front gun turret which was directly above him (this would account in part for Jack's training in gunnery), although this was not necessary on most operations. After the bombs had been released, the Bomb Aimer would take a photograph as proof that the operation had been completed. Some Lancasters had been especially modified to accommodate an RAF film operator. Jack's plane was one of these and although this operative was named in official records, no mention was made of how many times a special film operator flew with the crew. The Bomb Aimer could also act as a reserve pilot in the case of an emergency as he would have received some flying training.

The plane was cold and noisy. Their flying suits and boots were lined and bulky. The noise was probably a blessing in some cases as Jack notes in his diary that they thought bullets ripping into their fuselage from a fighter one night was flak. Small comfort.

The Crew
Col James: Pilot
Sandy Morrison: Flight Engineer
Jack Bewes: Bomb Aimer
Bill Fitzgerald: Wireless Operator
Peter Pettit: Navigator
Harold Humphries: Mid-Upper Gunner
Len Rosewarne: Rear Gunner

G. Harding: Mid-Upper Gunner. There is a contradiction between war records and the diary. The diary mentions that all of Jack's crew were Australian except Sandy who was Scottish, so it would appear that Humphries, RAAF, rather than Harding, RAF, was the Gunner. Harold Humphries is mentioned in Jack's personal diaries, Harding is not. The War Record is also confusing as the crew of any Lancaster was seven and not eight.

A W. Hodge also is mentioned in the War records as a passenger/joy rider. One possible explanation could be that Hodge was a photographer. The official War Records include F/L Hodge as a "joyrider/ passenger" on unspecified flights or flight. It was more likely he was an RAF photographer as 463 Squadron planes were especially modified to carry a photographer.

The Bomb Aimer was also routinely expected to take photos of the bombed sites. Jack spoke about the importance of these photographs as the sortie would not be counted as one of their 30 trips if the photo were not there to prove that they had dropped their bombs over the site.

Jack and the crew entered the war just prior to the phase that could be called "Normandy", as concentration at this phase of the war was to bomb sites around the Normandy area where the D Day landing was to occur on five beaches. This included bombing in the Pas De Calais area from where the "Buzz Bombs" were launched on London. While sites in Germany were still bombed – oil industry sites, installations, particularly railways, munition and industrial sites – the majority of his trips from 24 April to D Day were over France.

This crew completed thirty-five trips (sorties).
They were required to complete thirty.

Photograph taken prior to their last trip. What would their thoughts have been?

By 1944 bombing was strategic and methods for location of sites had been refined using different coloured flares and radar. The bombing of cities where there was industrial and political structure, shipyards and lines of communication was strategic, and the death of civilians could not always be avoided. International law at the outset of WW2 did not specifically forbid aerial bombardment of civilian area of cities. Indeed, the loss of morale that these citizens experienced as a result of bombing was deemed beneficial to the war effort.

HELLO ENGLAND

This story of young Australians shows their typical Australian sense of humour and understatement. This, together with the kindness and hospitality of the British people, carried them through every mission they went on and every loss of a friend.

The training Jack received in Canada at Edmonton – bombing, navigation, map reading, gunnery and oblique photography (showing various horizontal and perpendicular angles) – continued in England – aircraft familiarization and bombing.

The boys and the bicycle were shipped out of Halifax for Liverpool England and arrived in Lichfield in August 1943. They were excited to see London, a big city they had only heard about. They forgot that London was blacked out and stayed awake – to see nothing but darkness. They were sent to various bases in the countryside to continue more day and night training before arriving at Waddington, their Squadron base, in December 1943.

In West Freugh, the training concentrated on map reading, camera work and gunnery. Jack records other bases and areas over England that were used for practice, or for cross-country flights with simulation. There were flights over France ("nickels") to drop propaganda pamphlets urging the German population to abandon the war. While these "nickels" were valuable as training flights, many thought they were a waste of manpower.

They arrived at Waddington, their home base, at the end of December 1943 and after some further flying and bombing practice, on 20 January Jack's crew went on their first mission to Berlin.

Map showing routes of 463 and 460 Squadrons to Europe.

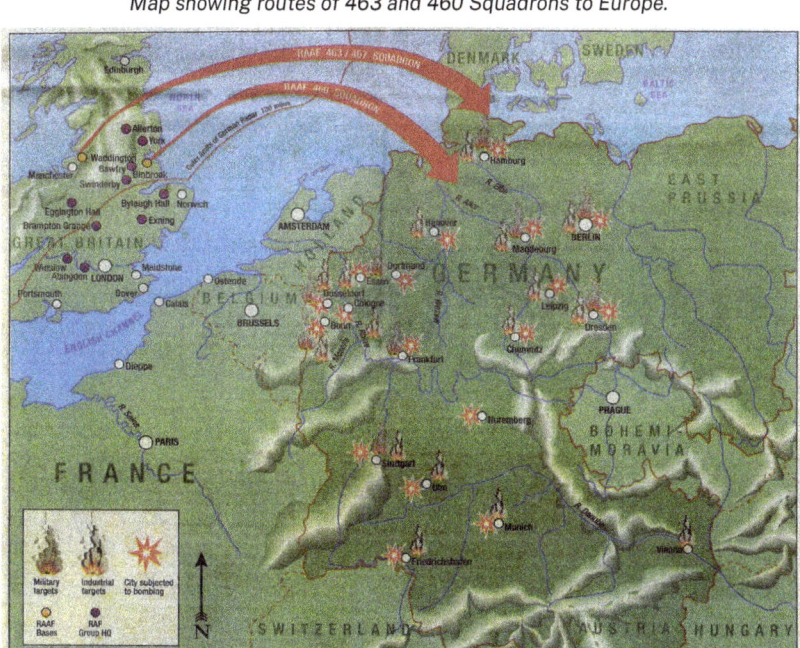

Legend shows military, industrial and city sites bombed.

NOT ALL WAR

From Jack's diaries, personal and operative, and his photos, it was evident that it was not all war or thoughts of war. These were young men and they had a young man's sense of fun. They would have had an eye for the girls and all women love a man in uniform. Joining the threads of these sources was not always easy.

Jack left Brighton, one mile out of Stannard, "the deadest camp he had ever been in", on 21 July. They had leave on the 27 and decided to visit Stannard town. It doesn't sound all that dead or perhaps Stannard town made its own fun. Jack and the boys went to *"the Shagger's or Virgin's Ball (as it was called). Roughest dance I have ever been to. Young (16) and old girls completely drunk and only there for one thing. Couples everywhere in paddocks on way home."* The boys decided to head home.

There was a period of leave from 1-26 August which they enjoyed. Len and Jack picked up "sorts". Jack must have had a few drinks. *"One night we picked up two sorts but as Len's one lived too far out of town, we picked up two (more) sorts at 10 (closing time) while they (the first two) were in the Ladies' room. Met my one next day at the Palais and boy I must have been drunk from the previous night as I still thought that she was beautiful but soon realised she wasn't. Dumped them as they had to be in by 10:30 (dead loss). Picked some more up at the Odeon but they were also dead losses".*

During this leave they visited Nottingham. They spent the first night in a dump in Queen Street. There was a fight two doors down. *"Next night we spent at Victoria Station hotel. Pokiest place in town. Had two married sorts in tow but..."* What happened there is a mystery as the page was cut from the book. It can be assumed it was either very memorable or not memorable at all. Either way it was not repeated as the boys enjoyed the next night, Friday, and their own company, *"half drunk. Composed songs. Great time".*

It appears from five entries in his diaries and in letters written to him, that Jack was a talented composer and solely missed by his mates when they were *"having a good time"*.

At West Freugh on the 28 of August there was further training – map reading, bombing, gunnery and navigation, primarily in Anson aircraft. Jack also received instruction in Wellington 111 fuel and oil systems, in parachute, dinghy and crash-landing drills.

This place did not impress Jack, *"Nothing to do except drink beer"*. They must have enjoyed themselves at this time as there are many photos of smiling and laughing "boys".

On 10 July, 1943, Jack and the boys were posted to Lichfield in Staffordshire where they got as far as Oxford by train. The train they were to take from there was cancelled and for some reason they could not take their luggage. They took another train but no further mention was made of the luggage. They had arrived in wartime England where there were last minute cancellations of probably many services.

Jack arrived at 27 Operations Training Unit Lichfield where he met Jeff Long. They *"played cards and drank all night"*. He and his mate Jeff stopped at "The Four Oaks" on the way back to Lichfield from Birmingham where, drunk and without train tickets, *"Jeff and I jumped from train to railway track"* to get back to camp.

Jack settled down into Lichfield where he met mates, some of whom would survive the war with him, some not. The five days between 22 July and 27 August are quite eventful. He was flying quite a lot, *"having plenty of experiences up in the air"*. They flew in Wellington aircraft where Jack was practising bomb aiming, gunnery, camera (photography). Some flights were to drop pamphlets over France. These "nickels" were regarded as practice runs for the bombing flights over Germany. He notes that his crew – Col, Murray, Pete, Len and Bill – were *"All decent blokes. Like sleeping, eating and drinking"*. This camaraderie would be necessary when they flew and cemented them as a crew.

During this time Jack met Ann, an Irish Roman Catholic girl he would become very fond of, at The Prince of Wales Hotel. She was with a Corporal who left her, so Jack took her home. They went out regularly after this. He was *"late for the first two dates but since then have been punctual"*. Jack must have been keen on her as he then was out with her six nights a week.

They celebrated Ann's 21st birthday on a Monday. Their young age quickly jerks one back to reality and to the realization that they lived for the day. It could be their last. It must have been a big celebration as *"Boy, was she drunk. A lot nearly happened but it did not. She was still sick the next day when she went on leave"*.

Jack received a telegram from Ann in August when her leave had finished to say that she would be arriving in Lichfield at 8:45. *"Raced like mad into town. No Ann. Got back to camp 11:45. Telegram was meant for Tuesday"*. *"Ann posted to Lossiemouth, Scotland. Finding out now that I really love her"*. Unfortunately Jack was unable to see Ann off when she left for Lossiemouth in September. By this time they had been going out for two months.

Jack and Maurie were good mates, best mates, and they went into town together. The Yanks had entered the war by then and *"have been buying us a lot of drinks"*.

Jack's Commission to Officer came through on 1 August 1943 and it was an opportune time to celebrate. He had four days leave which he intended to spend in London. He stayed two nights and one day as there were too many flying bombs. He says that there were hardly any the first night when he was drunk, but maybe he did not hear them. On the second night he was sober *"they sent 90 over. Boy, was I jumpy"*. Although the Blitz (from German Blitzkrieg: lightning attack) on London for 57 consecutive nights was heaviest in September 1940, the Germans again buzz bombed London from January 1943.

Their crew formed in Lichfield were Australian with the exception of a Scotsman, Sandy. Three were from Perth, three from Sydney. They began training on 8 August and were sent on sorties to drop leaflets over France ("nickels"). Col James is named as the pilot but none of the final crew positions are mentioned at this time.

The night of 9 September 1943 was not a good one for Jack and crew: *"Lucky to be alive today as last night was the closest I have ever been to death. During the night trip we were recalled to base owing to a heavy ground fog. While circling at 2,000 feet both motors cut and so Col put the nose down to pick up speed. We began to spin a bit but Col managed to level out at 200 feet. As both motors were going again we climbed but when we got to 1,000 feet we stalled and both motors cut out again. This time Col managed to level out again at zero feet. Lucky there was an altimeter lag of 30 feet and there we were tearing across the fields of Lichfield at 240mph and from zero to 30 feet up, fully expecting to hit something but God must have decided to look after us"*.

On 16 September 1943, Jack was hospitalised with the flu. However, he wrote: *"Nagged to get out in three days as I talked the nurse into faking my temp etc."*.

On 23 September, they went on another "nickel" and were over France for about two hours. *"A bit nervous at first but gradually calmed down. Eric was the Bomb Aimer in the other kite {plane} that went down but did not return. They must have wandered off course and were no doubt caught in the flak"*.

Jack's personal diary was a record of a typical life of young men of that age, wherever they might be in the world. There were good mates, girls and good times. It is hard to imagine flying on a sortie, not knowing if you would return or if the girls you had met and your mates from other aircraft, would see each other again. Life had to be lived on these terms.

Sometimes the girls Jack met and went out with seem to be around the same time. Ann, Maureen, Babs, Sheila – the mind spins trying to fit them in logistically. Being prejudiced I think Jack was a good-looking bloke, an excellent dancer with a sense of humour and an affinity for writing rhyme. So as his daughter I have no trouble believing that these young women were attracted to him.

Jack had not forgotten Ann. He had 18 days leave. On the 28 September he travelled all night to Lossiemouth to see her. He arrived at 8am. *"Went around and got Ann out of bed. Found she had booked a room for me at "The Rocky Bank" Hotel. Had a good time, especially at night."* He visited the Golf Course, though he does not record whether to drink, play or sightsee. Here he also visited Elgin.

October was an interesting month. Jack met Maureen and took her to the pictures. He thought that she was a nice girl, but she was not the only girl he was seeing at that time. His entry on 3 October mentions Babs and her mother Mrs. Colling. Jack had also met Sheila at the beginning of October. As he was an excellent dancer, it is not surprising that he and Sheila won the slow Foxtrot Competition at Castle Bromwich. He had been sent to "E" Flight where he says he was "bludging" because he was not sent on many sorties, although he was night flying.

Jack celebrated his 23rd birthday on 29 October. He had been two years away. He and his mates celebrated at "The Green Man" in Coleshill. It must have been a really good night. With no transport home, Jack and his mates hitched a ride on the back of a wagon, where they *"contracted a cold due to sitting on the back of a wagon with no overcoats. Could see hands turning blue".*

On his leave on 5 October Jack went to Ann's home at Sunderland where he met her brothers Pat and Oliver and her mother. *"Gee, they are a nice lot.*

Had a nice holiday. Visited her relations etc". In November he again visited Ann and her family for his two days leave.

The hospitality of the English families played a large part in the lives of these young men. For a while they had a home away from home. A thread of nostalgia and possibly homesickness runs through these entries.

On 15 November he had finished leave and was seen off by Ann. He left Newcastle by the 1:30 train for the small village of Morton Hall outside Swinderby to complete a Commando Course at the army camp there. Why a Commando Course for a flyer? However it was not all work. There was always time for fun. *"Met 'Jesse' James. Boy I had some fun with him and Jack Spratt at Callingham (Land Army) and Swinderby dances"*. The question remains, why a commando course?

Although not mentioned again in the diary, Jack and Jack Spratt remained friends after the war and must have spent some leaves together. Jack S lived at Nambucca Heads (NSW) and we had many holidays there as children.

On 28 November, Jack was posted to the Bracla RAF station in Scotland. He was sorry to leave Lichfield and was not impressed. *"What a dump. Cold as blazes and rain etc. Two parades a day, a quarter to 9 and a quarter to 2."* However there was still sightseeing to do on leave and life to enjoy. *"Went to Inverness with Tom and Smithy. Prettiest town I have ever been in. River through the centre, bridges connecting islands etc. Castle on the hill in centre. Ben Nevis, the highest mountain in Scotland in background. Went to a dance on Saturday night"*.

Life continued regardless of the war. November was an eventful month. This was when Jack met Doreen, a blond WAAF driver. It was attraction at first sight. Jack was constantly with Doreen and *"was sorry when she went home on leave"*. He had spent two leaves and two or three nights a week at Mrs. Field's (Doreen's mother). The Field home was truly his English home – he mowed the lawns and was encouraged to bring his mates to their home. He escorted Doreen's younger sister to dances. However, his feelings for Doreen are clear.

"Doreen at home (discharged from WAAF). She looks more beautiful

than ever. Wish she was not married". Jack and Doreen felt something for each other when they had first met, but it wasn't until after this Christmas that he knew that she was married. Jack doesn't say when Doreen married, only that it was just three days before her husband was sent to the Middle East. He respected this but still continued to see her.

How do the Catholic ethics on the sanctity of marriage of that era remain strong in the face of the uncertainty of war? For many, including Jack, it must have been a struggle indeed, and to what end?

This first Christmas in England must have been wonderful as Jack had been invited to Doreen's family home for Christmas and he, Bob and Maurie "buzzed off" to the Field's home. Before going to their home they met the family on the bus and went to the Green Man pub. It doesn't take much to imagine their feelings being in a family home again for Christmas. They were still so young.

"Gee, they had a wonderful home. Whiskey, poached eggs, duck, tinned peaches, gramophone, settee etc. Had a wonderful time and was sorry to leave".

The luxury of tinned peaches in wartime, a gramophone to dance to in a lounge room, carpet probably rolled up, and a settee. Good mates to share with. It brings home the more spartan life they led on the airfield and the simple comforts they had once taken for granted. There is nostalgia all through this entry.

The following entry underlines the tragedy of war.

"Maurie and Bill went on a trip with Bill Lawson and failed to return. Gee it was a blow to me as Maurie was my best pal. Hope they are POW's especially Maurie as his brother was killed last month in New Guinea. Eric arrived back in England ok".

Maurie was his best mate. Neither realised that this Christmas would be Maurie's last. It was unfortunate that two of Jack's original crew had stayed in camp one night whilst the rest went to a dance in Lincoln. Maurie and Bill were seconded to fly with another crew. They did not return. This would have been their first close war losses and the shock of the crew when they woke next morning, no doubt with good memories of the night before, to find the mates had bonded with were not there, can only be imagined. The adventure was over. Reality set in. We call it a tragedy if one friend we know dies. They knew friends that died daily, families who had lost all their sons. The knowledge that you might be next had to be faced. The effect of this on young men is the result of every war, unimaginable to the rest of us.

A lesson had been learned: Do not stay on Base if you have a 24-hour Leave Pass.

It is not clear if Eric was on that same plane. From Jack's diaries we are told that Eric was shot down, walked across the Pyrenees and managed to get back to England. He was shot down and killed on his next mission.

It was probably fortuitous that Jack left for Waddington 463 RAAF Squadron, on 28 December 1943. The base did not impress Jack, *"Lousy camp. All mud and slush. No showers or hot water basins on site. Parades every morning. Have been flying in both Halifaxes and Lancs"*. What a shock for the Australians, so used to good weather and bathrooms in their homes. The White Hart pub must have been a welcome stop for the airmen.

Life was a good few drinks and social life as the most was made of time off and comradeship. On 13 January 1944, *"all of the crew were invited to the Royal Observers' Corps annual party and boy did they have a good time. I did not know that they had gone as I had been at Newark."* He had gone to meet Doreen but *"the trams were late and I missed her"*. It sounds like he missed a good party as well.

The Aussie tradition of a good drink seems the norm for the crew. Why not? Tomorrow was never certain. Jack was cleaning the outside of the mid-upper guns when he nearly fell off *"as I was suffering from the previous night"*. There was the laconic humour *"Not on Ops thank heavens"*.

There was good news and plenty to celebrate two days before their first night mission. Their pilot, Col, got his Commission and they celebrated in true Aussie style. Jack *"had plenty to drink. In fact it is the drunkest I have been in a long time"*. There was a stage show wherever they went to celebrate. They met a lot of the local couples and other crews and all joined in the celebration.

THE REALITY OF WAR

From preparation and training for war, to reality. They started flying night missions over Germany. But reality was not with the crew at the start of their first mission to Berlin. Sandy was excited when he saw the distant lights of the flak. They soon realised that the dazzling lights meant possible death for aircrew of all squadrons.

The 463 Squadron's first flight to Berlin was on 20 January 1944, not long after the Squadron had been formed (25 November 1943). They would have been nervous, made even more so as they were a reserve crew, waiting to fly. With their new wireless operator, Bill Fitzgerald, a *"nice chap"*, they would not have known what to expect as it would all have been new to these young men. I don't doubt that they were nervous, regardless of the Miraculous Medal of Mary that hung in the cockpit.

"Cloud all of the way, Sandy (the Flight Engineer) got very excited when he saw some flak (anti-aircraft fire) 20 miles away. A scarecrow exploded about 200 yards from us over the target." The very bright "scarecrows" were a myth perpetrated by Bomber Command to reassure crews that these were flares fired by the Germans. Many were really their own Lancasters or Pathfinders loaded with guns, target illuminators and flares, shot down and exploding. Imagine the effect on the crews and their morale on their first flight if they had known that these could have been aircraft from your Squadron and that, at that very moment, men you knew had died by fire. Yet amongst all this light, the flames to guide you to the bomb target, the flak from the German guns, the burning targets, you still had your own planes flying in close formation around you dropping bombs, and at any time you could have become a "scarecrow" because of enemy fire, or because you had been hit by one the bombs carried by your own squadron. It was a good thing that these "scarecrows" were so bright. When over the target on the first Berlin mission, and with one exploding just 200 yards from

their plane, knowing that some of their own were dying in a burning pyre would have shattered their nerve on this first mission. Regardless of this, Jack records this as a quiet trip.

I think this would have been the only time that this excited Sandy or any crew member on their plane. Although in truth, it would have been spectacular, the many colours of the Wanganui flares, red with green stars, green with red stars, marking the targets to be bombed, the flak, the burning target, then the blinding flashes as a "scarecrow" exploded. Jack remarked *it was a "wizard sight"*. I doubt that he would have had this thought again as they were caught in flak for an hour over Bremen, with Col tossing the "kite" around and the Flight Engineer giving course-changing directions that had the Lancaster corkscrewing. This was no Christmas celebration.

"*Took off about 11 o'clock (Magdeburg sortie). Cloud again until we reached target. Half of it was clear, rest clouded over. Certainly was a wizard sight. Green and red TI's (target indicators) on the ground, Wanganuis in the air (red with green stars). Could see the city burning. Nearly missed target as PPF (Pathfinders) were late. Markers went down on the south side as we were level with target. Col turned straight in. Could see aircraft coming from the other direction. On the way back we were caught in flak for about an hour over Bremen, Wilhelmshaven, Frisians. Col kept tossing the kite around. Never thought they would stop tossing flak up at us. Sandy gave the best corkscrew I have ever heard when he mistook a Lanc for a fighter. Very happy when we got out over the sea*".

After this initiation into sorties, they were lucky enough to get a 48-hour Leave Pass. Jack and Len spent their time in London where they visited Madame Tussauds, The Tower of London, Parliament House and Westminster Abbey, no doubt fuelled by a few drinks along the way. The pubs, small, intimate, dark, so different to our bigger, light-filled ones, would have been a novel experience.

Three days later, on 24 February, Schweinfurt, the site of Germany's main ball-bearing manufacturing factories, was bombed the day after bombing by American B-17's. On the trip to Schweinfurt, another sentiment was predominant – relief that it was a quiet trip because of the cloud cover.

"As usual we flew over cloud but were always happy when those conditions existed as it meant no searchlights, which were always a menace. Over the target there was hardly any cloud but hazy conditions existed. The searchlight seemed to form a circle around the town with a break at each end".

However, with 35 Lancasters lost, it was not so quiet for others. Bomber Command tried a new tactic on this raid. The bombers were sent over in two divisions/waves. As well as Jack's plane entering the bombing area at the end of the town where there "seemed" to be a break in the other end of the circle of spotlights, he may have been in the second wave where only four bombers were lost rather than the first wave where 31 bombers were lost.

It is interesting that searchlights were regarded as a "menace", a very understated term.

The next trip, on 25 February, to Augsburg, was their fourth. Hard lessons had been quickly learned and put into practice. Previously they had made a straight run for the target, now they began doing weaving and banking searches on the run up to bomb the site which was in the fork of a river. This site was marked by red and green flares. They bombed, got the bombing photo and headed for home. The "mass of twinkling lights", the flak below, held no fascination for them.

"Another long but very quiet trip. The target was the best marked one to date. The town has a forked river in the centre of it and the red and green TI's were in one huge cluster in the fork. We made a good run and managed to secure our first aiming point photo. It was on this trip that we first started weaving and doing banking searches on the run up instead of straight and level as on our previous trips. As usual, plenty of flak over the target. It looked like a mass of twinkling lights".

With weak artillery defences, the aircraft component factory and engineering buildings in the northern and eastern districts of Augsburg were successfully bombed. Unfortunately the historic and beautiful old town centre was destroyed by the explosives and resultant fires.

On 1 March they bombed Stuttgart, an industrial city of military bases and a transport centre for Southwest Germany. One industrial complex was the Bosch Factory which produced components for the Luftwaffe, another the Daimler-Benz factory. The rail system was further damaged. The importance of Stuttgart can be understood by the years of Allied bombing from August 25, 1940 – April 19, 1945.

"Another quiet trip but as usual we were watchful as we were always expecting trouble. Supposed to have been decoys south of the target but owing to cloud we did not see them. Doubt that very much of the town was hit as it lies in a valley, with the result that it is very hard to pick up on H2S or G" (Radar systems used in the bombers).

Their Frankfurt trip on 8 March, 1944 was to bomb the railway lines and cut communication lines prior to D Day. This was successful as the railway yards, wagons and locomotives were destroyed and the lines cut. I am not sure how immured to war they were. It was their seventh trip in six weeks. Two Lancasters, ducking and diving, were "coned" by the searchlights. The comment was *"luckily for us, but bad luck for them"*. I imagine you concentrated on dropping your bomb load and getting out of danger – a form of self-preservation. Thinking about the others would mean loss of concentration and this could mean that you were shot down.

"Shortest trip to date but all the same very hot over the target and just after leaving it. Very hazy over the target but just south of it was clear as a bell. There was a huge belt of searchlights but luckily for us (bad luck for them), two aircraft were coned by them just ahead of us. Could see them diving and climbing like flies with flak bursting all around them. On the way back Len saw a combat on our port. Over the channel Sandy swore he (had) seen some chaps bailing out of a Lanc but were no doubt small specks of cloud as the Lanc kept going".

Hope or positively?

The following night, 9 March, they were sent to Marignane as part of 5 Group to precision bomb factory buildings. This trip was not without its highs and lows. The engines were being test run before take-off and the bomb catch, carrying 8,000lb of bombs, was accidently released by Page, *"Bags of panic"*.

Meanwhile Jack could not load the left-hand gun because the retaining part was bent. These "glitches" must have worried the crew. They may have thought, *"What else can go wrong?" Or possibly "Nothing else can go wrong on this trip"*.

With the preparation that had to be done for this trip, the buildings that had to be pin pointed, the moonlit night, which made it more dangerous as they would have been visible to the enemy and the difficult approach from the other side of the Bay, meant total concentration. This concentration could have had a calming effect on them (after the glitches before take-off) as they would have been really intent on their task. They hit their target and turned for home, without loss of any aircraft. However, the tenseness they would have experienced and their relief, could be summed up in the comment, *"it was beautiful on the way back as all the snow-covered mountains were glistening in the moonlight"*.

A bomb site (location unknown).

"A lot of preparation was necessary for this trip as it was a pinpoint job on a lot of factory buildings. Preparations consisted of lots of low-level night flying, orbiting certain points and bombing. The trip was done in bright moonlight at 8,000 feet. Had to orbit yellow TI's (Target Indicators) for at least half an hour. Only one searchlight over target which went out. But plenty of searchlights and flak over Marseilles. Could easily see the factories and airfield. Red spot (bombing indicator) was dropped right in centre of building. Had to make a time and distance run from a spot on the other side of the Bay. Page was shot up a bit over Marseilles. It was beautiful on the way back as all the snow-covered mountains were glistening in the moonlight".

And, while with silent lifting mind I've trod

The high un-trespassed sanctity of space,

Put out my hand and touched the face of God.

"High Flight" John Gillespie Magee.

"Pete flew for some of the time. Saw some lights which were no doubt French people signalling us. According to the photo we dropped our stick (ours was the best stick of bombs dropped by the squadron) right across the buildings".

At Marignane, although their bombs were dropped right on target across the buildings in this town, the relief and elation of this accomplishment was short lived. Something else did go wrong. On their way back the plane was forced to land at Predannack (Cornwall) on the South Coast instead of Waddington (Lincolnshire) in the North, as the Right Turret was "ropey". The forward position of Predannack Airfield made it a place for emergency landings. This base was used mainly for maritime operations and was particularly home to Mosquito planes which were used as ship escorts and to attack submarines.

The boys were tense before every trip. Perhaps Page typified this. He accidentally released 8,000 pounds of bomb while he was test running the engines before take-off and panicked the other crew. He was "shot up a bit" over Marseilles which is understandable. I would imagine the crew nearest to him would have calmed him as his nerves and the effect on the rest of the crew could have meant the difference between a safe return or no return.

Back at Waddington, there was a four-day break. It is not clear whether it was time taken to make the Lancaster flight worthy or because of unsuitable flying conditions.

Jack notes that their next trip to Stuttgart on 27 March was their longest, seven hours, because they had to fly over France almost as far as the Swiss Border before turning N-E to bomb Stuttgart. Their bit of bad luck of the previous trip seemed to follow them as they lost the starboard outer engine an hour before reaching the target. They had to then jettison two 1,000 lb bombs. They dropped them near a farmhouse that was lit up, but made sure they did not hit the farmhouse, just warned them that they needed to be in darkness. This shows the human side of Jack and these young men. They still had their humanity, but what long-term effect would this have had on the young men when humanity had to be turned off in order to carry out a mission?

When they reached the target, Jack spoke about Wanganuis (flares), but he noted that the enemy dummy Wanganuis could be distinguished from British ones as they left a smoke trail. They also saw enemy fighters reflected on the clouds below them and over the target.

"Had a bit of trouble this trip as we lost the starboard outer an hour before the target. Had to jettison a couple of 1000 lb bombs. Dropped them near a farmhouse. They soon turned their lights off. The enemy tried to trick us by firing up dummy Wanganuis but could easily distinguish them from ours as smoke trailed behind them. Saw a couple of fighters reflected on the cloud beneath us over the target".

Mission accomplished. Safe landing back at Waddington. Relief. Then their psyche was turned upside down. Two planes collided over the airfield – one was a crew that they knew well. Both burst into flames.

"When we arrived back at our drome one of our boys on his first trip and a kite from 1 Group collided over the drome. One burst into flames immediately, the other after it had peeled in. We saw it peel in as it was as bright as day. And boy, were we shaken."

Frankfurt was a German industrial town with metalworks and a river port. The first trip to Frankfurt on 18 March Jack noted as uneventful, although 99 industrial buildings were destroyed and the Opera house and the Medieval town were partly destroyed. The second trip on the 22nd killed over a thousand people and finished the destruction of the old Medieval Town, which had been one of the best preserved in Europe. The East Port suffered major damage.

"This was one of the best attacks Bomber Command ever put on, as the town was just about completely obliterated. Nearly collided with another aircraft over the target which turned in on us. Col backed off, so did the other chap. We could see his bombs falling out of his bomb bay as he turned away. At first I thought Col must have read my mind as I was going to ask him to turn left. Chewed a couple of wakey wakey pills just after we bombed and was air sick all the way back to base. Was not worried when Sandy thought he saw a fighter. Was as green as grass when we arrived at the crew room. Did not have an egg".

Jack was absolutely against drugs and this could explain his intense feelings. "Promise me," he said, "that you will never take drugs. Alcohol and cigarettes are enough". They were not thought of as drugs then. I can only think that the aversion to eggs at that breakfast may have been because of the memories they brought back, the mission and the physical feelings.

On 24 March the target was Berlin. The bombing of Berlin began in 1943 and continued until 1944. The 24/25 March raid was the last major raid on Berlin. Strong winds drove the bombers south and caused difficulties with the marking flares. The scattering of the bomber stream saw more losses to flak and to the German night fighters, particularly on the way home. The inaccurate marking of flares meant that the city, as well as small towns outside, were bombed. Industrial concerns and five military installations were damaged. Some aircraft strayed from their path and crossed "Happy Valley", the Rhine Ruhr industrial area which was heavily defended, resulting in more losses.

"A very tricky trip as regards navigation. I gave Pete a pinpoint on the way in over the coast. We were over the sea approaching the coast and he thought we were on the land. The result was that we had to fly right over Berlin for about 20 mins before we reached the markers. We were also against the stream and boy was the Master of Ceremonies (who directed all bombers) cursing us. The target was very hazy but very beautiful with all the different markers and flak. They were firing red flak at the MC so that the fighters or flak could get at him. On the way back, the broadcast winds were out with the result that 60% of the chaps crossed "Happy Valley". Luckily we went around the northern tip of it. We could see a lot of the boys coned and boy were they popping some flak up at them. Saw plenty of searchlights on the way back as it was as clear as a bell".

On 26 March, Jack records that the Essen trip was quiet. Forty-eight German factories as well as the town were successfully bombed. It is unfortunate to note that, amongst the civilians killed, a large number were concentration camp prisoners who provided the labour force for the factories.

"A very quiet trip. Thick cloud covered the whole route. The only menace was the contrails (condensation trails) by which the fighters could follow us. As usual the flak was very heavy but we expected that, as "Happy Valley" has always been notorious for flak and searchlights. Saw a couple of fighters after we left the target. Luckily they were going the other way".

On 30 March they bombed Nuremburg, an important infrastructure and economic hub. This trip may have been hard on the crew psychologically as they had a replacement navigator. Crews liked to keep all their original team. I imagine that this could have been because they all knew each other's work habits and anyone slow on the uptake could have meant that they did not return. There might have been a bit of superstition also.

Jack's diary of 30 March, and the comments that he has written of the trip to Nuremburg, testifies to a raid, that in hindsight, possibly should never have taken place. Normally raids were not carried out on moonlit nights but as there was a forecast of protective high cloud en route to the target, it was decided to continue, even though the Meteorological Reconnaissance Mosquito reported that the protective high cloud was unlikely but that there was the likelihood of cloud over the target. As well the high winds meant navigational difficulties and that the flares were off course. The raid on Nuremburg itself was a failure as there was little damage in Nuremburg. Many of the bombs fell near the Schweinfurt area.

"Kites shot down all around us near Ruhr. Fighters mainly. Flak. Expected attack at any minute. The hardest and most nerve-wracking trip to date. After crossing the French coast, the fun really started and lasted to the bottom of "Happy Valley". We saw a couple of kites go down and then we saw a Hun with his navigation lights on. When he started pumping cannon shells at a kite ahead of us my knees really started to knock. After that we saw plenty go down in flames. Although we were not attacked ourselves, we expected trouble at any minute as combats were two a penny. Things were a bit easier as we turned south from "Happy Valley". We noticed Schweinfurt lit up on our starboard. At the same time we saw the Wangunuis over Nuremburg. Most of the flak appeared to be on our port so I doubt if we really hit the city. Pete was sick this trip so we had a strange navigator but he was hot at his job. In all, 170 planes were lost or written off over ET (enemy territory), the rest over England. Brill (an airman on another plane) had a kite blow up ahead of him over England".

What went wrong, as well as lack of cloud cover, is not clear, but the flight plan of two straight lines of bombers over the Luftwaffe's major radio control beacons, without the tactics of evasion, bluff and feinting, looked suicidal to many pilots. The huge force of 795 Lancasters and Halifaxes was briefed on the flight plan: to fly to Nuremburg and back in procession. The opinion of this tactic was that, considering the size of the force, the fuel load that could be carried and the distance to Nuremburg, this was the only way the mission could be accomplished. However, if the weather forecast been accurate, Sir Arthur Harris said the raid would probably not have gone ahead. Churchill commented that the loss of 800 lives in one night was too high a price to pay.

Jack was on a ten-day break after this trip and may not have known that much of the bombing of Germany was over. There would never again be the consistent heavy losses in raids over Germany experienced from January to March 1944. Many of his next trips would be D Day pre-invasion raids against targets in the countryside and towns (unfortunately leading to many civilian losses), military camps, factories, gun batteries, radio and radar stations ahead of the D Day invasion force. These raids were a combined effort of Bomber Command, the American Eighth Air Force heavy bombers and Allied tactical day bombers.

Jack's diary changes prior to the Tours sortie from sorties exclusively over Germany to a combination of French and German area missions. Although the official date for when Bomber Command's targets changed to pre-invasion bombing over France is 1 April, missions in his diary show a mixture of French and German targets (Munich on 24/4, Schweinfurt 26/4, Duisburg 21/5). He does say the French missions were quiet in comparison to the German ones.

As noted in his diary on his next trip on 10 April, a quiet one to Tours, the target was communications. However, the crews were given an unrealistic command. These trips were "quiet ones" so Operations thought that they would count each trip as a third of a trip, meaning that three trips over France would only be counted as one, because they were "quiet trips".

The Aussie spirit kicked back:

"First of the French trips, object of which was to smash railway communications etc. as they were a hell of a lot easier than German targets. Our group decided to make us do three (trips) to make up one trip. All the boys kicked as they reckoned they would not go for a third of a row if they were hit. Luckily they changed it later to whole trips otherwise we would have been operating for years. Quiet trip with about three guns over the target".

On 11 April there was a 5 Group trip to Aachen. At this stage of the war, German targets were only attacked if conditions were favourable. Few risks were taken. In Aachen, railway and road, communications, and power supplies were damaged. Unfortunately, so was much of the town, including six hospitals. Jack's diary entry is interesting as it shows the favourable conditions and the work that went on behind the scenes (plotting of aiming point photos being just one) when the crews arrived back at base, and that flak seemed to be now regarded as "just something".

"Shortest German trip to date. As usual conditions were cloudy over France. Target was very hazy but could easily see the red and green TI's. Our photo flash failed to upload with the result that we had only fire tracks on our photo. However when these were plotted it turned out to be an aiming point photo. Besides usual flak over target, nothing of importance happened".

18 April, Juvisy (Paris). The attacks on 17, 18 and 19 April over France were to destroy railway yards. Jack notes only: *"Quiet trip. Bombing of Paris"*.

A "quiet trip" on 20 April. The railway yards at La Chapelle were bombed by Group 5. Here a new marking system, Oboe (radar) was successful. The bombing was extremely accurate and concentrated.

Jack notes that the trip to Brunswick (English name for the German city of Braunschweig) on 22 April was a "quiet trip", although this was a heavily defended city and it was the first time that a low-level marking system was used. The low-level cloud and the faulty communications between bomber controllers made this a largely unsuccessful trip. The city was bombed but so was the area to the south. The diary tells us a bit about the crew – Col "more short-tempered than ever". This is understandable as he was the pilot, and because of the cloud, was flying on instruments and had the safety of the crew resting heavily on his shoulders. The houses and civilians lost in these raids could not worry the crews. Many of these missions to destroy towns were to destroy morale of the enemy and the flight crews would have known this. It also shows the dangers from other planes in the group as "a few bullets" were pumped into their Lancaster from another Lancaster. This mission overwhelmingly shows what a big part luck played in their sorties.

"Back to Germany again on what was more or less a terror raid. Brunswick is supposed to have a lot of old wooden houses so we set out to burn it down. We mainly carried 500 lb American petrol bombs. Conditions were very hazy so Col had to fly on instruments. This made him more short-tempered than ever. This attack was entirely a 5 Group effort (Chop Group we were called). On the way back a couple of master beams caught us but they did not hold us for long. Our own PFF (Pathfinder Force) marked the target but they were not as good as the old mob, just one red spot fire which was hard to see as conditions were lousy over the target. Next day we found out that another Lancaster had pumped a few bullets into us over the target. We heard them hitting the kite but we did not worry as we thought it was only stray bits of flak, but they partially severed the airelon control wire (a hinged flight control surface usually forming part of the trailing edge of each wing of a fixed wing aircraft, used for imparting a rolling motion especially in banking for turns). If it had snapped on the way back, I doubt we would have reached base. As far as fighters etc were concerned, the flight was uneventful".

The trip to Munich on the 24 April was a story of luck and premonition, epitomising what war in the air was about. It was good luck they had to boomerang, bad luck a "nice crew" did not return.

"Boomerang in carb. Racing in all motors. This trip was our one and only boomerang (early return). Page (their crew member) flew as an extra (with another crew) on this trip and failed to return. Funny thing, all of them had a premonition that something would happen. Bad luck. They were a nice crew. We flew "W" which was the oldest kite on the squadron. We had to fly at 500 feet over France and climb to height as we approached the Alps. As we started to climb the carburettors iced up and we had to go into 'hot air' to keep the motors going. If we had tried to go on we would not have had enough petrol to reach base (use 100 gallons an hour in hot air). As we turned around another Lanc flashed underneath, missing us by about 10 feet. After that we were below the stream. Nothing exciting happened on the way back.

"Lucky we did not complete the trip as out of the four of us who had to bomb between 1,500 and 16,000 feet, we were the only ones to return".

This entry seems the epitome of understatement. The official report of 463 Squadron missions as recorded paints a very different story: "24/25, 4.44: In the Op (Operation) to Munich they had real trouble. Icing was so bad that all four air intakes iced up until the motors almost stopped. And the aircraft was losing height. At an alarming rate. They had to jettison the load and only regained control at 500 ft.".

As you read through these diaries, the effect of the war and the way in these men had to think to come through their missions and then to go back to what was once a "normal, ordinary life", seem impossible.

On 26 April they again bombed Schweinfurt, a nine-hour mission. At Schweinfurt the target marking was not accurate, there were strong head winds and night German fighters attacked in force. In spite of all that, there is humour in Jack's account, but humour born of tightly-wound nerves.

"On the way in we got a bit off track due to flak with the result that we arrived late over the target. There were plenty of searchlights and flak but luckily conditions were a bit hazy or else it might have been a smokescreen that the Germans often use. We weaved etc more viciously than we had ever done as we were just about the last kite over the target. A couple of searchlights flashed onto us but did not hold us. The town was certainly burning well and as we could not see the markers we dropped our load in the middle of the blaze. On the way back the winds increased from 30-90 mph (headwind) so Pete had to keep on revising his ETA. Col got annoyed as Pete asked him if he would like him to get out and push or just navigate. All very tired when we finally landed".

It would not be hard to imagine Col telling Pete to make up his mind or just get it right.

Col: "How far to the Coast?"

Peter: "35 or 25 minutes".

Later Col said: "How far?".

Peter: "25 minutes".

Col: "Why did you not give the correct figure the first time?".

Peter: "Col, we have just run into a 100 mile per hour headwind. By the way, would you like me to step out and push the bastard?"

End of conversation.

The sortie to St Medard-en-Jalles (a suburb of Bordeaux) to attack an explosives factory was their 22nd trip and the crew appears to be getting a bit jittery. Jack did note early in his diary that the key to returning safely was to check all parts of the aircraft thoroughly, and that nerves tend to go around the 25th trip.

"We were supposed to go ahead of the others and find winds but owing to our aircraft going DS (dysfunctional) at the last minute, we had to borrow one of 467's (Squadron). As we were late Col did not bother waiting for us to check much. Found out later that Len's guns were D.S. However we decided to risk fighter attack and go. Orbited yellow TI's on Bay of Biscay Coast for over an hour waiting for the target to be marked. As conditions were hazy PFF (Pathfinders) could not mark the actual target aiming point so we were told to return to base as it was a precision job".

They were sent back to bomb St Medard-en-Jalles the following night as they had not found their target.

"As next night was reported clear over target we went back to St Medard-en-Jalles. Flew over the sea most of the way. It certainly was clear so we went into attack at between 4-5,000 feet. The photo flares of the planes ahead of us made the target very clear and we could see figures running everywhere. Just before we bombed we were told to come up to at least 7,000 feet. However we decided to stop at our height and bomb and this nearly meant the end for us.

Just after we dropped our bombs somebody must have hit a dump and we were caught in the explosion and tossed everywhere. As we got out of that a machine gunner (Bofors) must have got onto us as small shells (like machine gun fire) started to whip past our nose. Luckily he kept firing ahead of us until we finally got out of range. Quiet for the rest of the way".

On 1 May, 5 Group was sent to Toulouse to bomb an aircraft assembly plant and an explosions factory. Jack calls this *"a quiet trip"*. The mission was successful and no planes were lost.

"Quiet trip except over target when rear turret hit by flak. On the way back, just before the French Coast, two fighters got onto us. One put his navigation lights on and cruised around us at about 1,000 yards. We had only 303 guns with a range of about 7-800 yards. Their idea was for us to fire at the kite with the navigation lights on. This would allow the second aircraft to line us up and blast us with cannon shells. Col wanted me to hop into the turret and fire at the first aircraft as he dived towards it. I told him to get lost".

After their break they were sent to Tours. *"A quiet trip. We went to bomb railway yards prior to D Day. Trips over France were quiet compared to German trips".*

On 21 May they were sent to Duisburg in Germany. Although there was plenty of cloud that night the marking was accurate and there was a lot of damage to the city. Although Jack calls this a quiet trip they orbited over the target for 12 minutes which must have been a stressful time as they could have been shot down before releasing their bombs. They would have become a "scarecrow". He attributes this to "someone up above". This is only one of Jack's references to his God throughout his diary.

"Back to Germany. As usual plenty of flak. On way back we wandered off course. Unless you were in the mainstream the German Ack Ack could pick your course, height and speed & blow you out of the sky. Someone up above must have been looking after us as they pulled the trigger about 30 seconds early. The shells exploded about 100 yards in front of us. You could smell the gunpowder. If they had waited, we would have been just another statistic".

On 22 May they were sent to bomb Brunswick where they again orbited the target. As "nothing exciting happened" I am wondering what classified excitement? Perhaps the chances of the "chop group" making it back were less than those of other squadrons – possibly because of dangerous targets and lower-level flying.

"Quiet trip except for predicted flak after leaving target and searchlights. Orbited target for 18 mins. Second trip back to Brunswick. This was a 5 Group attack as all the other groups had French targets. We were known as the "Chop Group". We seemed to cop the worst. Just the usual trip. Plenty of flak etc. Nothing exciting happened".

The sortie to Eindhoven on 24 May was to bomb the Phillips factory. There were only 59 Lancasters on this 5 Group mission. Jack's plane was recalled to base eight minutes from target. A Phillip valve is mentioned. This radio tube was used in radar and in communications from aircraft to ground operations. If missing, communication between Jack's plane and the Master Bomber would have been impossible. In any event the Master Bomber ordered all crews to return because of bad visibility. It is ironic that Eindhoven was the site of the Phillips factory which could have made the faulty valve.

"Quiet trip. Recalled to base eight mins from target. Phillip valve. All crew ordered to return from 51.44N 0439E. Dumped our bombs in the North Sea".

Jack was part of the Operations that started prior to D Day. The shorter trips were to targets around the landing areas. On 27 May they were part of a larger operation over Nantes, Bourg-Leopold, Aachen, Rennes as well as coastal batteries. 5 Group precision-bombed railway junctions and workshops in Nantes as part of D Day operations prior to 6 June.

"French trip aimed at destroying railway yards etc prior to D Day".

The next trips were all D Day preparations.

On 29 May was the bombing of railway junctions and workshops at Nantes. The 5 Group bombing (100 Lancasters) was so accurate that after 50 Lancasters had dropped their bombs, the Master Bomber ordered the other

50 to retain their bombs. Jack does not note whether he was one of the first wave of 50 bombers.

On 31 May, a railway junction and gun positions at Saumur were destroyed without loss. Jack's diary only notes *"bombing railway yards, gun positions prior to D Day"*.

On 3 June, as part of a 5 Group mission, Cherbourg and Ferme D'Urville gun positions and a German signals station were bombed. The signals station had to be destroyed as it was near the coast chosen for the invasion. On 5 June, Pierre du Mont on the Cherbourg Peninsula was bombed.

Jack notes in his diary that these were prior to D Day which suggests that the crews knew of that operation.

In a letter (newspaper and date unknown) "RAAF Squadrons in D Day Bombing", D. Bruce Otten, President of 464 and 466 Squadrons writes:

I quote from the RAF Bomber Command News: "In the early hours before dawn on D Day RAF Bomber Command attacked 10 heavily defended coastal batteries with maximum operational strength. Details of all Squadrons... include the RAAF heavy bomber squadrons – 400 Sqdn Chisbecq, Maisy, 463 & 467, St Pierre du Mond Sqdns. In these attacks 1,159 aircraft dropped 5,258 tons of high explosive and 28 tons of incendiary bombs.

They bombed St Pierre Du Mont and Argentan on D Day (5 June,1944) which I assume was the one operation. Jack's Lancaster was one of those bombing the coastal area in preparation for the D Day landing.

"Quiet trip. Chased by two fighters from target to coast. Bombed about 5:30am. Had we gone below the cloud we would have seen all the troops landing. Glad we did not as the warships fired at all aircraft below cloud level. Would not have known what hit us."

This mission was significant in that it was their 30th trip, the number they were required to do.

They escaped the fighters, relieved to have done so on their last mission, but when at base they were screened and told they had to do five more.

The diary records the human side and some typical Aussie humour albeit black:

"*Thought our luck would not last. All aircrew were obliged to do 30 ops (providing they survived), have six months off and then do a further 20 trips with a different crew. If they so desired, they could do 45 straight ops and then not be required to fly unless they volunteered. Very few crews got to 30, let alone do more. As we had worked well as a crew we decided to do the 45*".

On 19 June, after nine days leave, they were to bomb Watten. Standing by for three days waiting for cloud to clear would not have done much for their nerves, only to find when they got there that conditions were still too cloudy for efficient bombing of the flying-bomb store (storage of buzz bombs that fell mainly on London). They *"were bombing ahead of the invasion troops, then recalled as Ops cancelled"*.

On 21 June they were sent to the Ruhr (Gelsenkirchen) where the accuracy of this bombing raid ensured that all production at the oil plant targeted stopped. *"Another trip to Germany. Bomber Command no doubt thought we were getting too many easy French trips. Usual flak etc. Hit by very heavy barrage flak. 46 kites shot"*.

This trip to the Ruhr was much more eventful and the possibility of being shot down was brought home more so than on other trips when the Flight Engineer, Sandy, who was seated next to the pilot, thought he was hit. This was close to Jack also who was possibly lying down directing the pilot to the bombing site, rather than seated if operating the front gun turret. *"Flak through Col's Perspex. Sandy thought he had been hit. Down everywhere. Reminded me of the Nuremburg trip"*.

On 23 June they had a quiet trip to Limoges but their trip the following day to Prouville was hard. They were to bomb railways, gun positions etc in support of invasion troops.

"Hard trip though only to the French Coast (Pas de Calais) 50-75 searchlights. As soon as an aircraft was coned down it went in flames. Supposed to be our last trip. All were jumpy".

Their first four extra trips were OK but on their fifth extra trip, on 27 June, to Vitry-de-Francoise, they all were understandably "Jumpy as hell". They were supposed to fly at 17,500 feet and a course of 240 degrees on the second leg (no explanation of what "second leg" meant).

"When we turned onto the second leg the Germans had put up a box barrage between 17-18,000 feet. (A barrage is a continuous firing of weapons. A box barrage is a gun barrage on three sides or more surrounding a given area to prevent aircraft escaping enemy fire). *I asked Col was he going to go above it. He just said, we are flying at 17,000 (feet). I then asked him to go around the barrage but he said, 'We have been told to fly a course of 240 (degrees)'. We flew straight into the barrage and did not cop it. Flak hit the windscreen. Sandy thought he had lost his head. I told him he must still have it as I had never heard of anyone talking through their neck.*

When we finally got back we told Col to tell our C.O. that we were not flying anymore. He tried to convince us to go on but we just said nothing. As far as we were concerned, Col had had it and we would rather complete our tour later.

Ops not too bad if you are lucky and fairly efficient, besides treating every one as your first, which is the main thing, because if you are over-confident you have had your time. Nerves definitely on edge every trip. Although you don't realize it, they do go at about 25 trips.

Jack's Operational Record (as per his diary):
35 sorties: *214.33 hours.*
Longest trip: Schweinfurt 9 hours 8 minutes.
Jack's last flight was on 27 June 1944 to Vitry de Francoise.
Total bomb load: 178 tons 530 lbs. (161,719.28 kilograms).
(He did do one further flight from Lichfield on 25/7/44 but details of this are not recorded).

Official Australian War Memorial records quote "F/O James DFC and crew had a fairly straight tour of 35 ops. Ops only record them as having trouble twice". Very clinical.

The diary tells another story. Jack was entitled to six months leave as he had completed his tour of duty which it appears he did not have. *"I went to 27 OTU Lichfield to do my six months"*. The dates of his last operational flight, 27 June, and the first flight at Lichfield (Training Unit) on 25 July, 1944, gave him barely a month's break.

This section is barely recorded and what is recorded is unclear. The diary does not note whether any of these extra five flights were outside England, only that the five sorties were dual bombing and they were of short duration of 1.05 hours to 2.15 hours between 25 July and 15 October 1944, on Wellington Aircraft.

"When that was over I was sent by mistake to the centre where newly finished aircrew were sent prior to their six-months break They told me they did not know what to do in my case and to come back in two days. When I returned they said that they had some bad news i.e. I would be going back to Australia. I went to Brighton. On the train from there to Liverpool we were held up for 30 minutes in London (signal failure). Rockets were landing. I thought just my luck for a rocket to fall on the train".

Jack's God looked after him to the end. If he had not been sent to a centre that did not know what to do with him, possibly because he did not have the six month's break, he may have been sent back to do further trips with a different crew and possibly a different result.

He was "lucky to be here".

LETTERS WRITTEN BETWEEN AIRMEN

These letters are revealing of the unreal world of war and of the humour and caring of the men who wrote them. The planes, 'kites", are spoken of with affection. They are personified, have a life of their own – *"the beaut kite no longer lives here – it went the way of them all ... wouldn't it rip you!"* The crew was missing, but the tone seems to be one of sadness and acceptance.

Aussie humour and optimism comes through very strongly. They are "browned off" by the "big wigs", a mate's heart problems are referred to as more likely "excessive use of grog". Bathing is often mentioned. In one instance it is "excellent". In another diary entry Jack laments the lack of showers and hot water. Commentary on the weather is common. One letter writer comments that once they leave the cold winters where they couldn't even play sport, they would probably come home to "flood or drought".

They were lucky to have English families who cared about them and shared their family lives and thoughts with them. Everyday topics were spoken about and this normalcy would have been a solid and comforting thing. Sheila, the young daughter of the Field family, signs one letter as "Love from your young sister".

The letters the airmen wrote to Jack reveal a lot of their feelings and their way of dealing with the war and the constant deaths of people that they knew. Some were cheerful and future plans were made to meet up. The uncertainty of life was pushed away. They described life on the bases and the activities there. Others talked about letters written to mates with no reply, with writers left to wonder whether their mates were still alive. Regardless of the content, humour runs throughout.

But no amount of humour can hide the courage, hope and bravery that shines through.

Jack was a prolific letter writer. He wrote to his mother and his grandmother fortnightly, and to his sisters, Joan, Hazel, Beryl and his brother Fred on a regular basis. These letters were recorded as answered so there was regular family correspondence. There were regular letters to Joan Hobson, the WAAF (enlisted in the Womens Auxilliary Air Force) he had worked with in Sydney and to a Molly French who was not mentioned in his diaries. It also appears from his correspondence, the people letters were sent to, the scattered locations throughout Australia, that he may have written to the families of airman he knew who had been killed.

The postscript that Sheila Field added to a letter that she had written to Jack on 23 February, 1944 asks: "Have you written about Maurie yet?"

This mention of his dead mate seems to confirm that he had sent letters to the families of friends and fellow airmen who did not return from their missions. He had said that he had never been to Bondi, yet he wrote to a Mrs. King at Bondi. Other unfamiliar names are Mrs. Pinch at Double Bay, Mrs Corcoran at Kingsford.

All letters vary in how these men coped – most with Aussie humour and understatement.

The tone of this first letter is cheerful:

1/7/43   Aus 423699

Sgt Fraser A J. RAAF
11 Porc. Grand Hotel,
Brighton.

Dear John,

Back from leave yesterday and have been going like hell ever since.

50 of us have been posted to the army for 12 days. All to Armoured Divs. Running around in tanks and guns won't be too bad.

We leave at 8 am tomorrow so excuse shortness of note.

All photos enclosed, hope you are satisfied. They worked out pretty close.

I hope you, Eric, Reg and the rest of the boys are all doing ok.

No more, all the best,

Regards from all,

"Chook".

P.S. Have written to John but as haven't got your number, have addressed envelope to Reg.

"C".

Another letter full of understatement and optimism. In this letter "things were a bit grim" as apparently a few of the boys have not been able to be contacted. Although "Old Jack" was supposed to suffer from nerves and heart trouble, Eric, in a typical Aussie way, puts it down to "excessive alcohol", a problem many would have when they came home.

5/8/44
A423579 F/S Anderson E. J.
c/- RAF Station,
Snaith. Nt. Goole, Yorks.

Dear Johnny,

Well mate I have been on a Squadron a week today. Arrived last Saturday evening, signed at various places on Sunday, did three circuits and bumps on Monday, a cross country on Monday and my first trip on Tuesday. So you can see they didn't waste much time.

It's a pretty good joint and I don't mind stopping around here for a while if things stop as they are. A fellow gets a bit browned off sitting around and waiting through while the big wigs discuss whether we are likely to go or not.

Say, do you ever hear from Gordon Armstrong at all? I have written twice now and so far there has been no reply. Sounds a bit grim doesn't it?

Had a letter from Eppy a while back. Apparently he has got a few in now. He told me old Joe Marks was a F/L now with about 29 up on P.F.F. Ruin a fellow wouldn't it?

By the way, I am due for nine days leave on about the 28th of this month so let's know where you hang out. It's almost eleven months since we met last.

Hope you got to Lichfield, it's a good station and also would be handy for me to get to you as I have relatives in Birmingham.

Gosh promotions ruin you on these joints. Some blokes are F/S one day, P/O the next and F/O on the day after. My boss is an F/O right now.

I saw Oscar Furniss' name and also Bill Thayers on the casualty list a while back so apparently a few of the boys have been buying it.

You were saying you were due for a RAAF gong; I believe I am also so maybe will apply for it sometime. Old Jack our ex-W/OP sports it and a wound stripe though where he got the wound I am buggered if I know. When I last heard he was on a station training to do A.C.P. duties. (Air Crew?) He is supposed to suffer from nerves and heart trouble. The former is most probably caused by the excessive amount of grog he drinks. He packs a terrific line of bull now according to his letters.

Les Dowling has been a squadron leader for a few weeks now but so far I haven't heard from him so don't know how things are.

Well mate, this is all for now, drop us a line sometime before the 28th.

Your old cobber,

Eric.

The following letter was written by Jack. Did he still have it because Eric had "bought it" or could not be located? Perhaps it was returned to sender.

25/8/44
A423600
P/O Bewes J.J.
Officers' Mess,
RAF Lichfield Staffs.

Dear Eric,

Just a short note to let you know that I will be going on a few days leave shortly.

I had promised the rear gunner quite some time ago that I would spend a leave with him otherwise I would pop up and see you.

I will be back here on Friday 1st June so if you could get up here any time after that I will be around. Hoping to see you round about that date. You should have quite a few up by now.

All the best of luck mate,

        Your old pal,
        Johnny.

Had a letter from Betty Stinson the other day.

J.

The following letter from Bon is interesting in that many names appear to be in code and in the way that the loss of the plane and crew are described. The loss of the crew is understated and reads sentimentally. The news of the mates, Bob, Len, Col, Pete, Joe and Wanny reads factually. Possibly another way of dealing with war? There is the usual air of optimism and the plans for the future.

> Aus. 22823.
> Cpl. Spewey B.A.
> 170 N Flt.
> R.A.F Stn.
> Wadd.
> 21.11.44
>
> Dear Johnny,
> To-day I came into dinner & fair dinkum, received a hell of a shock when I saw your letter lying on my bunk. Only last week I was thinking how you & the boys were doing & I fully intended writing to give you my address but, you beat me to the punch & I'm mighty glad too. It is great to hear from you once more & to know all is well with you up there.
> Johnny, I'm sorry to have to tell you this but the beaut kite no longer lives here, it went the way of them all about three weeks ago on its 63rd trip. Wouldn't it rip you? The skipper that night was a guy named O'Reilly with an

Aus 22823
Cpl Freney B A.   T/OW Flt.
RAF Stn.   Wadd.

Dear Johnny,

I came in from dinner and fair dinkum, received a hell of a shock when I saw your letter lying on my bunk. Only last week I was thinking how you and the boys were doing and I fully intended writing to give you my address, but you beat me to the punch and I'm mighty glad too. It is great to hear from you once more and know all is well with you up there.

Johnny, I'm sorry to have to tell you this but the beaut kite no longer lives here, it went the way of them all about three weeks ago on its 63rd trip. Wouldn't it rip you! The skipper that night was a guy named O'Reilly with an all-Aussie crew except the engineer, and I was sorry to hear they were missing even apart from the old faithful kite. It was a funny thing. I told the skipper he was to leave it at U's (?) disposal as I have the two camera kites to look after, Y and the old L (now V) so I reckon the old X must have heard me and took a dim view of it. However she did a good job, Morris finished his tour in her, so I guess she doesn't owe us much. Unfortunately we didn't have time to put a couple of stars up, also the two "gongs", but I have a snap of her with Jg (?) and when I get some more printed will let you have one.

Yes, Johnny, it would seem as though you boys picked a hard time to do your tour. Morris did the 30.

At present Wanny is away on nine days leave – official – and I have hopes of clearing out for the same time early next month. Seeing as I had such a good time in Glasgow, I'm willing to try it again. The cold weather has got me bluffed a bit though I guess I'll survive.

How is your weather up there? Ours has been on the nose lately and we even had a slight fall of snow last week. I haven't been on the grog much lately, bed has a special attraction for me these chilly nights and usually crawl into it early. I haven't played any sport for months. This is a lousy country for winter sport isn't it?

I haven't heard from Bob, but some time ago did hear a report that he was in Kodak House when a buzz bomb landed nearby and as a result is suffering from the effects still; his nerves have gone and he is in some home or other. That is how the rumour goes but don't know if it is true.

I am glad Len got his commission. You will all be together again now eh? One night Wanny and I came home from the camp pictures to find Col playing poker with the boys in the billet. He was wearing "the gong" then and I was very pleased to hear Pete made the grade. What about you, boy, any chance of you getting one too? If I had anything to do with it, I would give all you buggers one.

There is still nothing definite about the boat. I am quite resigned to spending the winter here as you are. I reckon we are in for a beaut. Just my luck. While I was in the East we had a record summer, now this. Ten to one when I do get home a guy will run into a flood or something. From all accounts they are having a drought out there now.

I think that about covers all I have to report this time, chum, so will sign off. Give my regards to Len and Fitz, the boys wish to be remembered to you all, Joe is still going strong, cheerio Johnny, all the best,

    From your old cobber,

    Bon.

The letter from Sheila Field (Doreen's sister, who was 16 at this time) tells us a little about how life continued in war time Britain.

Bacon End Stores
Old Chester Road, NA Coleshill
Birmingham.

Dear Johnny,

Just a note to enclose the snaps that you and Col ordered. Mr. Mayne developed your film but I am afraid they haven't turned out too good. The ones you took at Bacon's End are O.K. but the others, you just can't make them out, still perhaps you will sort them out & let us know if they suit.

How is life at Camp these days? It's pretty dull at B.E. I am feeling a little tired at the moment after the dance last night – it wasn't a very nice dance. The Band was super, but only the usual parties were there, including the "Mcract" so on the whole it was pretty rotten – and not one of the boys could compose a song like you. We dragged Doreen to the dance and she was very pleased about the fact that I won a spot prize – 20 "Churchman No 1". She reaped the benefit of that.

Have you been to your Victor Silvester Dance, or is it tonight?

Tell Col that I have been playing the new records a lot, especially "Ain't that a lot like love" and "Do you know why", I have really gone crazy over that record and also please inform him that I object to being called "Shirley", as he sent his love to "Shirley" at the bottom of one of his letters to Elsie.

Well as I said this is only a brief note so I will sign off now and write properly in a day or so.

Best of luck.

Love from your young sister,

Sheila.

P.S. Have you written about Maurie yet?

It appears Sheila could write prolifically as well, if the length of this "short" note is anything to go by.

Mr Field, Elsie Field, Col James (the pilot), Mrs Field, Sheila Field, Jack Bewes

18/12/44
Officers Mess,
RAF Station
Morton-On-Marsh, Gloucester.

Dear John,

Sorry I have not dropped those snaps back before this. Glad to know that you are on a boat list soon. I have been posted to the above address, but it is not that extra bad.

Arrived here on the 16th and everything so far is ok. I have slipped into a nice easy job. The billets are ok and the bathing excellent.

Well John I wish you all the very best of trips home. Cheerio and all the best of good luck.

Your old pal,

Syd.

Doreen sent this picture to Jack and wrote on the back:

Happy Landings Johnny,

always,

Doreen

Doreen Allan, née Field

THE PROPAGANDA BOOKLET

The Ministry of Information was formed in London on 4 September 1939. Its functions were to produce domestic material for enlistment as well as propaganda material as a source of psychological warfare. Propaganda leaflets and booklets were generally dropped by plane. These missions were called "nickels" and were often used as training flights for the Air Force.

The atrocities committed were illustrated and described in 10 different languages and distributed in the form of cartoons, leaflets and booklets. All were truthful, factual representations of atrocities. They were dropped in all invaded countries – France, Holland, Belgium, Yugoslavia, Denmark, Norway, Poland, The Netherlands, Luxemburg, Greece.

The leaflets had many purposes. Some were to convince the population of occupied territories not to support the German war machine. Others were to weaken the morale of the German people and troops. Those dropped in concentration camps were to give the prisoners hope that the war was about to end. Many were picked up and read although the penalty, if caught, was death.

The first page of the leaflet that Jack had among his papers shows Chamberlain and Hitler shaking hands above the caption *Why is there no Peace with Hitler?* The following pages then graphically illustrate why.

The opening pages show attempts that were made to broker peace, pictures of Jews marching for relocation, concentration camps and then of them labouring in mines.

Why is there no Peace with Hitler?
Chamberlain meeting with Hitler prior to Britain's entry into the war.

The atrocities by the enemy committed are shown in graphic detail:
- In Yugoslavia a 15-year-old boy hangs from a lamppost;
- Soldiers of the SS amuse themselves desecrating a church;
- A widow, Eugenia Wlodarz, and student Elizabeth Zohorska, are sentenced to death for spying;
- A Russian student, Zoya Kosmodemyanskaya, is tortured and killed – "one of thousands".
- Women being marched through "Death Forest" to be shot. There were no men left.
- In Greece, a picture of a family – men, women and children – dead with their mouths open. They had starved.
- On 1 September 1939, there is a picture of sisters doing field work who came across the dead after 10 hours of strafing by Germany.

- In Denmark a patriot wearing the red, white and blue Danish scarf is in agony after being bayoneted.
- A group of people fleeing with their animals: "Whether from Norway, Holland, Russia or Greece, all the streets in Europe have mothers and children fleeing. They are like a drop in the ocean".

The pamphlet concludes with three points:

    1. Hitler broke every peace promise he made.

    2. Hitler cold-bloodedly prepared for war for a long time to conquer and enslave Europe.

    3. Hitler perpetuated, in every land that he occupied, atrocities that had not been known for hundreds of years.

PEACE with Germany – YES.
PEACE with Hitler – NEVER.

It is doubtful that these messages had any effect on German citizens, but the night missions were relatively free of any losses and were considered valuable as training flights.

TRAINING AND WAR

Air Force

Date of birth: 29.10.20   Date of Enlistment: 25/11/41

Date and Place of Aircrew Selection Board: Sydney. 25/11/41

Medical Category: A1 B.A.B.

Date of last Medical Board: 25/11/41

    The men trained under The Empire Training Scheme were fortunate in that they were given extensive training in Australia, Canada and England. Their early missions from England to drop pamphlets were relatively safe and were regarded as training flights. Even while on active service flying sorties, they continued training flights over England – navigation, bomb aiming and gunnery practice.

Courses Attended:

Date	Place	Marks
7/12/42 – 19/2/43	Lethbridge Canada Bombing and Gunnery	72%
7/12/42 – 19/2/43	Lethbridge Canada Bombing and Gunnery	74%
7/12/42 – 19/2/43	Edmonton Canada Bombing and Gunnery	80.8%

Results of Training Courses

Lethbridge:
Anson Aircraft. 7/12/42-19/2/43: AB Initio Bombing Course.
41 hrs – 71.8%

Lethbridge:
7/12/42-19/2/43 AB Initio Gunnery Course.
8.5 hrs – 74%
Air to ground targets from various sections of aircraft.

Tests:
- Night Vision (Average)
- Altitude Tolerance (Above Average)

Edmonton:
26/2/43-1/4/43: Map Reading, Bombing, Photography, Handheld Obliques (a determined line of sight, i.e. to target).

Edmonton:
22/2/43-1/4/43: Air Observers' Navigation Course. Anson Aircraft.
35.55 hrs – 80.8%

West Freugh, Holyhead, Ballyhalbert, Little Ross, Bardsley, Rhyl, Ballyquintin, Caernarvon, Moffat: 28/6/43-19/7//43: Map Reading with Bomb Aiming, Map Reading with Auxilliary Gunnery, Infra-Red Bombing.

Anson Aircraft. 96.45 hrs during day; 29.5 at night.

Comment: "Needs further practice experience but has the ability to do well".

West Freugh:
22/6/43-17/7/43: Gunnery course. 3.2 hrs.

Lichfield:
Certified that I have received instruction in the Wellington III fuel and oil system and that I thoroughly understand the operation of this system and manipulation of the control.

It is certified that I have received instruction in and fully understood the following crew drills:
1. Parachute Drill.
2. Dinghy Drill.
3. Crash landing Drill.
96.45 hrs Day, 29.5 hrs Night.

8/8/43-10/1/44:
Various bases and courses prior to first mission over Berlin 20/1/44.

Exercises on Wellington Bomber over:
Woodhall Spa, Bishops Stortford, Trowbridge, Wittering, Ragdale, Baggots Park, Base, Catterick, Malyon, St Neots, Mowsley, Braintree, Kelso, Harrowgate, Goole, Sudbury, Duxford, Okehampton, Wallingford, Bardsley Island (Wales), St Tudwalls, Huntingdon, Haltwhistle, Feltwell, The Smalls, Cannock, King's Lynn, Land's End, Linsdale, Peterborough.

Bases: West Freugh, Lichfield, Winthorpe.

Hours: August 1943: 166 hrs 40 mins

September 1943:
137.35 hrs during day, 67.50 hrs at night.

Bomb aiming by Sim (simulated) bombing, live bombing, camera gun, air firing, feathering. 120.30 hrs day, 29.5 night.

Note: F/O Col James appears to become permanent pilot on 8/9/43 after being one of various pilots on above practice sessions. He alternated with Hamilton, Rodgers, Cooper and Green 8/8/43 – 10/1/44.

Exercises on Halifax Bomber and Lancaster "F" and "R" Bombers: Familiarization, bombing and simulated exercises. One plane lost on these exercises, fire in outer engine.

Hours: 159.35 day, 82.5 night.

Waddington, Lincs – Home base for 463 RAAF Squadron.

October 1944: 93 Group ABI's Course Hixon

Operational Aircraft	Squadron	Hours
Lancaster 111 & X	463	265 hrs 22 mins
Lancaster	1661 C.W.	29 hrs 5 mins
Halifax	1661 C.W.	7hrs 10 mins
Wellington etc.		214 hrs 20 mins

Date of Last Sortie: 27/6/44

Number of sorties: 35 (plus one from Lichfield over France).

Last Operational Command: Bomber Command 5G.P.

Total Operational Hours: 214.33

Total Flying Hours 515 hrs 57 mins.

OPERATIONS AND REMARKS

Note: These recorded here were only the trips across the Channel. There were also local exercises for various reasons, air/sea firing, and bombing recorded at Wainfleet (Airfield).

At Waddington, from their first sortie to Berlin on 20/1/44 to their completion of 35 sorties on 27/6/44, their bombing sorties over Germany and France were interspersed with training flights within England. There were 199.19 hours spent training and 214.33 spent flying sorties. The training was at Wainfleet and Epperstone for bombing; air-sea firing at The Wash on the East Coast near Wainfleet, air test flights and formation flying over various locations.

The bombs carried were of two different types – heavy bombs and incendiaries. Under the Lancaster directly below the Bomb Aimer's bubble was a long unobstructed bomb bay which could take the larger bombs – 8,000lbs (93,629.74 kgs), 4,000 lbs (1,814.37 kgs) 1,200 lbs (544.31 kgs) plus incendiaries. No other plane carried such weighty explosives.

N.B. The record of planes lost is from Jack's diary. The numbers vary in some instances from the Operational War Diaries compiled by Middlebrook and Everitt.

35 sorties completed. 214.33 hours flown.

Total Bomb load: 178 tons, 530 lbs. (plus one extra sortie).

Official losses from Jack's Squadron: 69 aircraft in combat, 10 crashes on landing.

FLIGHT LOG BOOK

(Conversion: 2.205 lbs = 1 kilogram)

Date	Place	Duration (hours)	Bomb Load/ Remarks	Losses (planes)	Sortie No.
20/1/44	Berlin	7.30	10,650 lbs	35	1
21/1/44	Magdeburg	6.23	11,180 lbs	55	2
24/2/44	Schweinfurt	8.50	10,288 lbs	35	3
25/2/44	Augsburg	7.5	10,420 lbs Aiming point photo taken.	24	4
1/3/44	Stuttgart	8.30	9,800 lbs	4	5
9/3/44	Marignane	9.30	9,000 lbs Low level flying. Aiming Point photo taken.	0	6
15-16/3/44	Stuttgart	7.58	9,970 lbs Lost starboard motor hour before target.	40	7
18-19/3/44	Frankfurt	5.42	12,170 lbs	22	8
22/3/44	Frankfurt	5.36	12,778 lbs	33	9
24/3/44	Berlin	7.07	11,600 lbs	74	10
26/3/44	Essen	5.04	13,800 lbs	9	11
30/3/44	Nuremburg	7.52	10,780 lbs	94	12
			Nuremburg was the biggest single air battle of the war. More than 800 aircrew were killed and 170 aircraft destroyed or written off.		

Date	Place	Duration (hours)	Bomb Load/ Remarks	Losses (planes)	Sortie No.
10/4/44	Tours	5.56	14,252 lbs Aiming Point photo.	1	13
11/4/44	Aachen	3.44	8,976 lbs.	9	14
18/4/44	Juvisy (Paris)	4.36	14,600 lbs Aiming Point photo taken.	17	15
20/4/44	La Chapelle (Paris)	4.37	9,000lbs Aiming Point photo taken.	12	16
22/4/44	Brunswick	6.35	8,900 lbs.	42	17
24/4/44	Munich	6.05	7,900 lbs Boomerang trip. Carburetor Icing.	30	18
26/4/44	Schweinfurt	9.05	8,788 lbs	29	19
28/4/44	St Medard-en-Jalles (Bordeaux)	7.28	12,380 lbs Bombs not dropped.	0	20
29/4/44	St Medard-en-Jalles	7.26	11,380 lbs.	0	21
1/5/44	Toulouse	7.29	10,890 lbs. Aiming point photo taken.	10	22
19/5/44	Tours	5.30	13,500 lbs.	7	23
21/5/44	Duisburg	7.29	13,500 lbs.	30	24
22/5/44	Brunswick	5.50	8,000lbs.	35	25
25/5/44	Eindhoven	2.55	14,400 lbs. Ordered to return. Bombs dumped in North Sea.	0	26

Date	Place	Duration (hours)	Bomb Load/ Remarks	Losses (planes)	Sortie No.
27/5/44	Nantes	5.10	14,800 lbs. Aiming Point photo.	27	27
31/5/44	Saumur	6.15	13,500 lbs. Aiming Point photo.	10	28
3/6/44	Ferme D'Urville (Cherbourg Peninsula)	3.35	13,500 lbs. Aiming Point photo.	0	29
5/6/44	Pierre Du Mont (Cherbourg Peninsula)	4.25	9,500 lbs.	0	30
6/6/44 D Day	Argentan	4.45	13,500 lbs. Aiming Point Photo.	0	31

Planes in snow, 463 Squadron

**Screened then told we had five more to do.
Thought our luck would not last.**

Date	Place	Duration	Bomb Load/ Remarks	Losses	Sortie No.
19/6/44	Watten	2.10	13,500 lbs Recalled. Op cancelled.	0	32
21/6/44	Ruhr (Gelsenkerchen)	4.20	11,250 lbs	46	32
23/6/44	Limoges	6.20	9,400 lbs. Aiming Point photo		33
24/6/44	Prouville	3.15	9,400 lbs.		34
27/6/44	Vitry de Francoise	7.30	11,400 lbs Aiming Point photo.		35

A record of the ops would not be complete without mentioning the controversary surrounding the Nuremburg bombing on 30 March 1944. Even though the weather was unsuitable, with protective cloud unlikely on the flight but cloud over the target, a huge force of 795 planes, (572 Lancasters, 214 Halifaxes and nine Mosquitos) were to fly to and from the distant target in two straight lines over the Luftwaffe's control beacons. They were not to evade enemy fire using any tactics. To the crews the flight plans looked suicidal. To Air Ministry officials they looked uncharacteristically bad.

The size of the force, it is also argued, made this formation necessary as any planes that deviated from the main force would be picked off by the Luftwaffe. To raid and get home in daylight without further losses meant that direct flying was necessary. This was the deepest raid into enemy territory and the fuel carried was only enough to fly directly there and back.

Eight hundred lives were lost. It was the biggest loss of any sortie of the war. To Churchill, the loss of 800 men in one night was too high a price to pay, even if Nuremberg was the living symbol of Nazism.

Map showing extent of bombing sorties over Germany by Jack and crew.
The targets were military and industrial areas and cities.

FOR ALL THE BOYS WHO DID NOT RETURN

Last Landing

Off this earth I leave behind

And soar God's heavens

Till our stars I find

And fence the towering clouds

With others of my kind.

Fear not if I should lose my way

Nor keep, keep sad thoughts for my returning day.

Tis that! I flew the Heavens

Too high and reached

God's guiding hand and

Heard him answer to my cry,

Your journey's done – NOW LAND.

From *The Bomber Boys* by Bomb-Aimer Sgt. Alfred Burford Sleep.

90 Squadron, Lancasters.

Written 28 August 1944, two days before he was killed.

"RAF Lost Half of All Bomber Crews"

"Air Chief Marshal, Sir Arthur (Bomber) Harris said today that nearly 50,000 British bomber crew personnel, out of a total of 110,000, were killed during the war.

The fact that the combined losses of the British and Canadian armies from D-Day to the end of the war were less than the 50,000 showed what these RAF men had endured.

The casualty rate, which the lads accepted cheerfully, was greater than anything I find in history among a similar body of men, over a similar period.

Their sacrifice was not in vain. They reduced Germany to chaos and helped to end the war more quickly".

(Air Chief Marshall Sir Arthur Harris; newspaper clipping. "RAF Lost half of all Bomber Crews" Salisbury, Rhodesia. Date and paper unknown).

IBCC Digital Archive,
accessed December 19, 2022,
https://ibccdigitalarchive.lincoln.ac.uk/omeka/collections/document/33773

Total RAAF bomber airmen killed in action: 4,149

LIFE AFTER THE WAR

As a civilian, Jack's acceptance of life must have been the same as that of many returned personnel. Although the memories of what they experienced must never have really faded, somehow they gained some peace leading what appeared to be a "normal" family life. But underneath the façade the scars ran deep.

When he returned to Sydney in February 1945, Jack, with six other returned servicemen, was sent to Melbourne to train as an Enemy Aircraft Spotter. By this time General Douglas MacArthur and the Americans were in Australia, mainly stationed in Brisbane. Things were grimmer than many Australians realised. The Japanese were close. A "mythical" Brisbane Line from Brisbane west was devised whereby Australia would be defended south of this line. (Conjecture still exists over the true facts – did this line really exist or was it to exist in the event of invasion?) Thankfully MacArthur decided Australia would be defended in New Guinea.

After his training Jack was sent to Tamworth N.S.W. where he met Pearl, a nurse at Tamworth Base Hospital. Pearl was from the small country town, Guyra, just north of Armidale on the New England Tablelands. Pearl had a great sense of humour, known for joining in or instigating a bit of mischief. She enjoyed life but had a practical streak that Jack probably needed. She would have recognised the neuroses beneath the surface.

Jack was discharged on 19 March 1946 with the rank of Pilot Officer.

They married in Tamworth in March 1946 and moved to Sydney.

Jack and Pearl bought a home at Beverley Park, in the St George area, near a golf course and Kogarah Bay. At this time he was working for Government Stores as their Storeman. This was a very good job and involved buying everything needed for all Government Departments in NSW. Jack had strong principles and this was a job where, on many occasions, he refused suppliers who offered incentives. He had had trouble with a solicitor when buying his home, but more stressful than this was that his home was under a flight path. The noise of the planes was constant and he couldn't take it. The effects of the war still plagued him.

He applied for and got a job at the Forestry Commission (now Parks and Wildlife) as a clerk and took a position as First Clerk at Glen Innes on the Northern Tablelands and then transferred to Baradine in the Pilliga Scrub (Forest). Maybe his memories of Tamworth where he was stationed as enemy aircraft spotter and where he met Pearl, his wife, held peaceful memories for him. He settled in with his family and his two children, Lynette and Garry. Ian was born at Glen Innes.

To us, life was the same for all the families around us – playing, school, mischief. But things were not as we children saw them. As a young girl of no more than nine, I remember my mother worrying that my father would return home safely by train to Baradine from one of his many journeys to Sydney where he was studying "Personnel Management" (HR I would imagine it is termed today). Regardless of the mental problems he was having then, Jack never complained, was grateful for every day, and I can still see the pride and enjoyment he displayed in all his achievements. These ranged from woodwork – making a desk, bookcases and tables, to building a barbeque through to his academic achievements. The help and advice he gave to others in the Forestry was probably the greatest of all his achievements and what he enjoyed doing most. He truly regarded himself as "Lucky To Be Here". Each day, each activity, was a gift.

Jack had always been a talented tennis player and he and Pearl spent their Saturdays playing competition tennis and Sundays were spent playing social tennis. Saturday nights were open house and all our friends were welcome.

We grew up having parties, barbeques and music. It was more than a happy house to many who walked through the open door, it was a second home. The war had taught him to enjoy and value every day and the people who were part of those days.

Jack and Pearl passed on their enjoyment of living life to the full every day, of taking pride in all achievements of children and grandchildren. But Jack's forte was people – he always had time for them and their problems. He listened, advised and acted.

I think a fitting memory of Jack would be a comment made by a Parks and Wildlife Ranger in Somersby (Gosford) Forest in 2006, after I asked him if he remembered my father, Jack Bewes, ten years after his death and eighteen years after his retirement: *"He was a legend. He helped me when I started work and everyone he met. He won't be forgotten"*.

What an epitaph for a life well lived.

JACK'S WIFE PEARL

Jack described her as a "pearl" and that it what she was to him and to all of her family.

In her youth Pearl was a mischievous girl who got up to all sorts of pranks around Guyra, her hometown. One example is the story of the Guyra ghost, a myth that has gone down in history. According to Pearl the ghost that haunted this house on the Armidale edge of Guyra was a group of kids, herself being one. As she grew older she loved her tennis and horse riding and from her photo album it is evident that she did not lack for "beaus". She was an attractive woman who caught Jack's eye while she was nursing in Tamworth. They married and whilst in the country she fitted into the community and gave Jack the support he needed over his difficult years of adjustment back into post war life.

Pearl was an intelligent and capable woman. When the family moved to Sydney, she joined the workforce as Storewoman at Goyan Control, a manufacturer of machine parts in Padstow. We did not appreciate at the time that she was the first Storewoman ever in Sydney, responsible for audits and for ordering.

When Jack retired they travelled overseas and enjoyed a full life when back in Sydney. They played competition and social tennis and golf. The family surfed at Cronulla with Jack's mother many Sundays. They both enjoyed their grandchildren and spent much of their time with them. Pearl's help and love for these children was inestimable and the love she gave was fully reciprocated. Jack's health deteriorated in his seventies but he still led a fully active life, mentally and physically. She kept an eye on Jack's health and was with him when he died, nineteen years after his retirement.

Her strength of character was extraordinary. She lived independently, cooking her own meals, washing, baby-sitting, at her home until her death at ninety-three. The garden was not neglected, nor were the birds that flocked to it.

Two of the lasting memories she has left are an image of her sitting on the back patio in the evening, where she sat so often with Jack, she with a brandy and soda, Jack with a scotch and soda. Or of her in her favourite chair in the lounge room conversing animatedly with her children, grandchildren and later great grandchildren. She and Jack shared the trait of listening.

When we think of Jack, we think of Pearl, the woman who stood beside him, a strong and equal partner throughout their relationship.

Pearl, 1944, a nurse at Tamworth Base Hospital

GLOSSARY

Bofors: The Bofors 40mm gun is an anti-aircraft autocannon designed in the 1930's by Swedish arms manufacturer A.B. Bofors. Its range was 23,490 feet.

Brisbane Line: Myth or fact? This line is shrouded in conjecture. No official record of it exists. Eddie Ward, Minister for Labour and National Service in John Curtin's Government made the allegation that this was a line drawn across the top of Australia West from Brisbane. If attacked the northern territories would be abandoned to Japan. This allegation was backed up by General Douglas MacArthur, Supreme Commander of Pacific Forces. This plan had earlier been submitted in a different form by Lt General Mackay (GOC of Australia's Home Forces). A Royal Commission concluded that no such documents existed.

Buzz Bombs: These were German V-1, "Vengeance", weapons used primarily on London. They looked like small aircraft made of sheet metal, with loud engines, short stubby wings, propelled by a simple jet engine that ran on 80 octane gas. Bright exhaust flames trailed behind. The sound was like that of the buzz from a Model T engine. When the "Buzz" stopped, the residents of London had about 12 seconds to reach cover.

Churchill, Sir Winston: The British Prime Minister from 1940-1946. Then again from 1951-1956. He was famous for his inspiring speeches and his refusal to admit defeat.

Coned: Caught in searchlights. When the searchlight caught one plane, all the other searchlights would focus on it (cone it) and all the flak (barrage of fire) would concentrate on this one aircraft.

Crew: A Lancaster crew consisted of 7 men.

Dam Busters: The common name for 617 Royal Air Force Squadron. There were nineteen Lancasters in the Squadron. On 16-17 May 1943 special "bouncing bombs" developed by Barnes Wallis were used to breach the walls of three of the Ruhr Valley dams. The success of "Operation Chastise" led by Wing commander Guy Gibson was marred by the loss of 53 airmen killed, three captured and eight aircraft destroyed. Two hydro-electric stations were destroyed, factories and mines damaged and destroyed, 1,600 civilians killed. The German war effort was hindered until September 1943.

Empire Air Training Scheme: Britain realised that it did not have enough air crew to maintain the Royal Air Force. The Dominions were asked to provide personnel. Most training was conducted in Canada. Australia undertook to provide 28,000 aircrew, 36% of the total needed. The Scheme effectively ended in October 1944.

Feathering: When the blades on a variable pitch propeller can be rotated parallel to the airflow to stop rotation of the propeller and reduce drag when the engine fails or is deliberately shut down. (This term is borrowed from rowing.)

Flares: These were Target Indicators used to guide the bombers when they were at the target. Different colours were used to light up the target area. These had the code names New Haven, Parramatta and Wanganui. These names were chosen when three Bomber Command personnel were asked where they came from. One man was from Newhaven, England, one from Parramatta, Australia, one from Wanganui, New Zealand.

> Newhaven: Red, green or yellow. Used when there was some visibility over the target area.

Parramatta: Generally red or yellow ground markers usually dropped in clear weather. They were guided by the ground-scanning H25 radar system.

Wanganuis: Red with green stars, green with red stars. Christened "Christmas trees" by the Germans. Usually used when the target was obscured by cloud.

Flat Flares: A decoy flare to prevent a ground missile homing in on the plane. As the flare is hotter than the engine, the missile will home in on the flare.

Photo Flares: To aid the Bomb Aimer photographing his hit.

Group 5: A specialist operative group formed between 1943 and 1945, led by Air Vice Marshall Sir Ralph Cochrane. It was called 5 because it comprised aircraft of five airfields of which Waddington was one. Jack and crew flew as part of this specialised force. 5 Group is best known for the Dambusters Mission.

Happy Valley: Slang for the Rhine Ruhr Industrial Area.

Harris, Sir Arthur (Known as "Bomber" or "Butcher"): Marshall of the Air Force. Responsible for the saturation bombing of Germany. A controversial figure in that he insisted on this when others in the Ministry thought German oil supplies should be targeted.

Kite: General term for an aeroplane. Lancaster.

Pathfinder Force: Elite Target Marking Squadrons led almost every raid over Europe and often flew on their own. They flew 51,053 sorties of the 360,056 sorties flown during the war. Operating between 1942 and 1945 the PFF changed the fortunes of the war for Bomber Command. They located and marked targets with flares so that the bombers following could bomb with greater accuracy. This could not have been achieved without the PFF, the majority of whom were RAF, with airmen from all Commonwealth countries, who had completed a considerable number of operations. At first PFF crew were volunteers.

Rankings: P/O Pilot Officer; F/O Flying Officer; F/L Flight Lieutenant; F/S Flight Sergeant; W/O Warrant officer.

Radar: There were three systems: Oboe, H2S, GEE.

> Oboe: This system was used to mark targets for heavy bombers and for direct attacks on targets. A pair of radio transmitters on the ground sent signals to a transponder in the aircraft. The Pathfinders used Oboe to drop their flares. Oboe could only guide one aircraft at a time. As these navigational units were limited, the flares were dropped and the Master Bomber (directing all planes to the target) would then direct the Lancaster as to which flare they were to aim for. If flares were dropped off target, the Master Bomber would direct the Bomb Aimer to bomb the colour of the most accurate indicators. Flares also indicated turning points for the Bombers on approach and after dropping the bombs.
>
> H2S: was the first airborne ground-scanning radar system to identify targets on the ground for night and all-weather bombing. The area below showing landform features was mapped. Used in the Battle of Berlin because Berlin was outside the range of Oboe. It was the most accurate of the three radar systems.

GEE: A radio navigation system. It measured time delay between two radio signals to produce a fix (locate the target). Accuracy was from a few hundred yards to 350 miles. GEE was the first hyperbolic system to be used navigationally (1942-1970).

Squadron: A group of planes. A Lancaster Squadron consisted of 7-10 planes.

Target Indicators: Used by the RAF Pathfinders. These flares were small bomb cases set to burst at a certain height and containing candles – red, green or yellow – which ignited and continued to burn over the target for up to seven minutes. They were normally dropped by Pathfinders to provide easily seen visual aiming points for the following bombers. (See also flares).

Toilet: This was an Elsans (named after the manufacturer). Basically it was a bucket with a seat and cover. If used above 10,000 ft, the airman had to also use oxygen from a portable tank whilst using it. It was prone to tipping over as the aircraft manoeuvred to avoid enemy air fire. Hated by both crew and the ground staff who cleaned the plane. Crew avoided using it as much as possible and one solution was to bring one's own bottle.

WAAF: Women's Auxiliary Air Force.

Wainfleet: An RAF weapons range on The Wash on the east coast of England, near the town of Wainfleet. During WW2 it was used by Squadrons to test the Stabilising Automatic Bomb Sight on bombers. The site was controlled from a control tower and targets included old ships.

Wound stripe: Originated in WW1. It was originally a small strip of gold braid, then a brass strip badge.

REFERENCES

Australian War Memorial Records. Canberra Bomber Command Crew Museum. Nanton, Alberta, Canada.

Charlton, Michael. Historic U.K.

Cornell, John, T. Editor-in-Chief. Air Force Magazine. March 1, 2020.

Cox, Sebastian. "Sir Arthur Harris and some Myths and Controversies of the Bomb Offensive". Speech given at RAF Historical Society, June 17, 2009.

Goodwin, Paul. *The Last Navigator*. Allen & Unwin. Australia, 2020

International Bomber Command Centre Digital Archive:
https://ibccdigitalarchive.lincoln.ac.uk/

Middlebrook, Martin. (1973) *The Nuremburg Raid*. Pen & Sword. UK, 2020

Middlebrook, Martin and Everitt, Chris. *The Bomber Command Diaries*. An Operational Reference Book 1939-1945. Pen & Sword. UK, 2020

NAA (National Archives of Australia). A1134.77/AIR (No 467 Squadron) Pathfinder Force – Technique, Barcode 304281.

Newspaper Articles

Partridge, Eric. *Dictionary of RAF Slang*. Penguin Books. UK, 2016

Wikipedia

OUR MEMORIES

Children's memories of their fathers differ but some of our memories are constant. Jack was a man who always had time for others, a man who loved friends around him and who always gave unstinted time and love to his family.

Lyn's Memories

My memories of my father were of the reliable kind man who was always there. We talked so much. During these talks he passed on his values and beliefs and I have tried to live by them.

When we lived in Peakhurst we walked to the station at Narwee every morning to catch the city train. I just recall talking without pause but the subjects elude me except for two conversations. One must have been about drugs:

"Promise me you will never take drugs. Alcohol and cigarettes are enough". These were not considered drugs in the 60's.

"I don't like talking to people who are ignorant or stupid," I said on another occasion. Dad was not happy.

"Treat everyone the same." he said. "You don't know what has happened to them or if there is something mentally wrong".

He had time to listen to everyone at the Forestry, where he worked as Personnel Officer, and to us and our friends. He always had someone who wanted to talk with him. He never disappointed – he could talk the leg off an iron pot and the telephone should have been a permanent appendage as part of his ear. His ability as a storyteller was legendary, as was his humour.

There was another side to him. He derived satisfaction working with his hands. He was a meticulous worker and so pleased and proud of his achievements. He built me a desk to study at, bookcases for our rooms and an occasional table. The brick barbeque, in the corner of the yard near the back fence, was the *piece de resistance*. It was quite large with a box for storing wood on one side and a cupboard for implements on the other. Across the top was a metal plate and here he would hold court, barbeque fork in one hand, beer in the other and always someone to talk to.

To me, my father was the man I walked and talked with, met in town every Friday afternoon for a drink with him and his work mates before we both continued on our separate ways. He was the super dancer I loved whirling across the floor with. He was the man who was so proud of all I achieved and I the daughter who was and still is so proud of him, his achievements and his wisdom.

Thank you, dad, for being such a huge part of my life and leaving a legacy of wisdom and kindness that I try to pass on to my children and grandchildren.

Garry, Lynette, Ian, 2008

Garry's Memories

I do not have a lot of memories about our years in Glen Innes (1948-1955) other than Dad having to dig the snow away from the rear door in the winter months and having visitors who were probably in the RAAF with him.

We left for Baradine in 1956 and lived there until 1959 when we moved to Sydney. Mum and Dad used to take us to the woolshed outside Baradine on Sunday afternoons to go roller-skating whilst, no doubt, they socialised by having a few drinks with the other adults. Dad and Mr. Brennan (the District Forester and our next-door neighbour) organised a bonfire every year for cracker night in June and we invited the neighbours and their kids.

The highlight of the year was the annual holiday at Nambucca Heads where the Forestry Commission had a cottage on the headland within the State Forest. Dad would pack up the Morris Minor for the trip to the coast. He drove there in one day. The cottage had no electricity, no town water and a fuel stove. There were no separate bedrooms but there were about eight single beds on the verandah. The toilet was a pit toilet in the bush about fifty metres from the back door, often frequented by snakes and spiders.

We would swim daily at the beach at the bottom of the cliff. We would get there by walking down a bush track and over the sand dunes. The beach was unpatrolled but we had dad and other adults so we swam without any worries. We had many memorable holidays at Nambucca Cottage.

Dad was transferred to Sydney in 1959 and built a house at Peakhurst. We completed our school years there and we would walk with dad to Narwee station where he caught the train to the city and we would get off at Kingsgrove. In 1960 we started tennis coaching which led to Saturday morning comp and dad took us most days. This led to the 1980's playing competition with dad and his mate Bob on Sunday mornings in a team called "Hangovers". These were a memorable number of years as dad was a very good player.

The backyard at Peakhurst holds some special memories with mum and dad. Every year on Christmas Day they would have an "Open House". There were Christmas drinks from about 2pm for anyone who wished to come.

Everyone brought their drinks. Mum provided the barbeque and snacks that went on until midnight. Those who could still stand then found a space on the lounge room floor or on the back lawn. Dad was the centre of attention, telling stories and enjoying a whiskey and beer before he disappeared to bed.

1971 saw mum and dad do an overseas trip with some friends to England and Europe. This was his first big trip on a plane since the war and he was very uptight and nervous at the airport. He had a wonderful trip and caught up with his wartime friends in England, especially the Field family. I feel that he came home a more relaxed person.

Dad retired from the Forestry commission in 1980 and enjoyed 19 years of retirement travelling and being with his grandchildren.

He was a truly remarkable person and I could not have wished for a better father.

Ian's Memories

Baradine – We were living in Baradine when I was about seven years old. Dad would make arrangements to take us to Nambucca Heads for our holidays. We had days filled with fishing and swimming. We stayed in the Forestry Cottage on a headland very close to the beach.

My High School Years – I wagged my first week of high school at De La Salle Kingsgrove due to the cruel treatment of the Brothers who taught us. They used the strap, keys and a whistle to hit any student who misbehaved. If we left our hats on when entering the classroom we would get hit over the head with these objects.

I had been wagging school for two weeks when the police picked me up and returned me to the school I was avoiding. Dad spoke to me, just us. When I explained why I wagged school he understood and supported me in the meeting with the Brother in charge of the College. Once I returned to the classroom one of the Brothers called me a clown and sent a letter home. Dad was not impressed and arranged a meeting with the teacher. Once that meeting was over I received an apology from the teacher.

Work years – I was 15 when I received my first pay packet. I gave Dad a One Pound note and told him to have a beer on me at the pub. I really wanted him to have a beer on me because I felt he deserved it for all he did for me over the years. Years later, when he told me how much it meant to him that I had done that, and how special it was to him as I was the only child to do that for him.

Tennis and sports – Dad, Garry and I played Sunday morning competition tennis when I was about 14 years old. I remember winning the match with Dad, the last set being a 23 – 21 marathon. We won five sets to four. It was a great day and holds a special memory for me.

Dad also took me surfing at Cronulla Beach when I was about 12 years old. I had a rubber surf-o-plane and he would push me off with a wave. He would do this for hours with me.

Anzac Day and Dad – On Anzac Day every year, Dad, Garry, myself and friends would go to Burwood RSL. He would watch the Anzac March (he only walked it once himself) after going to Church. Then we would all go for the afternoon show at the RSL which he really enjoyed. Dad NEVER talked about the war.

WWII and Dad – My father was SO BRAVE during the war. He and his crew flew 36 missions over Berlin and Europe with RAAF Lancaster Command 463 Squadron. Very few crews survived such a large number of missions. I am so proud of his outstanding bravery, courage and devotion to his country and the part he played in ending the war.

Mum told me how similar I was to Dad as we always helped people during our lives. During Dad's personal and business life he always helped people where possible. I am glad to say he passed this trait on to me. I have followed my father's example and have worked with different charities for the homeless and people in need of help and support.

I love my Dad and am so proud to be his son.

Thank you, Dad, for giving us such an amazing life and family.

The Grandchildren

Jack and Pearl had seven grandchildren, and eleven great grandchildren. The greatest sorrow in Pearl's life was when she buried a grandchild, Nathan, who was killed in the Afghanistan War.

Danielle's Memories

As Jack's eldest grandchild, I was old enough to remember Pa's stories, and he was old enough to be able to tell them. Time had eased the trauma of what he and his mates went through serving in the Royal Australian Air Force, Bomber Command.

As kids, my sister, brother and I spent many weekends at Nan and Pa's. Nan would teach us how to knit and sew as we watched the tennis of an afternoon. Pa would teach me cursive writing so that I did not have to lift my pen, and how to type on his old typewriter. They both taught me a love of gardening, and also taught me, my sister Kate and brother Brian, how to putt. Pa would put a cup on the lawn and we would see who could get the most balls in.

Pa, or Jack I called him as I got older, inspired me to do many things. I studied Latin, because he had done so at school. I played tennis, because of his encouragement, knowing what a great tennis player he and the rest of the family had been. Although I did not follow his hints on taking up ballroom dancing, I stuck to ballet as my preferred dance style. He and Nan sat through every one of my concerts, which meant a lot to me.

Pa told me of the bursary he received, one he could not take up, as he was had to go straight into the workforce after High School to support his family as his father had died. Throughout my High School years, he and Nan were always interested in my studies and full of praise when hearing of my marks. Before the HSC started, they both sent me a telegram wishing me 'Good Luck', and other words of encouragement.

Once I had left school and could drive, I would go over to Nan and Pa's house for dinner and stay the night. Before dinner Nan would have her brandy and Pa his scotch – I would alternate between the two, some nights having a brandy, some nights a scotch. For dinner, Nan would cook steak and onion gravy or her famous Sea Pie, and along with a few Chardonnays, they would tell me many stories of their younger years living in Baradine and Glen Innes, and their move to Sydney. I loved hearing Nan's stories of growing up in Guyra, and her nursing days in Tamworth.

My love of Modern History meant that I had a keen interest in World War II, so I would ask Pa what the war was really like. He would tell his remarkable, fascinating stories, interspersed with his dry sense of humour, around the kitchen table at 1 Iraga Avenue, his and Nan's place, or at our house.

I hope you enjoy the stories in this book as much as I did listening to Pa tell them. These stories will you give you some insight into what these men, and, indeed, all our armed forces went through.

Mum, thank you very much, for penning Jack's stories to paper. They will not be forgotten.

ACKNOWLEDGEMENTS

The writing of this book has been a grieving process mixed with the unexpected uncovering of the human side of war. It is the human side, the courage and the understatement of the men just "doing a job" that I was most interested in telling. The textbook of war has been written so many times.

An enormous thank you to Jacqueline Buswell who edited many times and unfailingly called me to task when I thought that all was okay. "All is not okay". The emails, questions and comments were never ending – until now. A friend and a professional.

Thank you, Jan Cornall, who heard my stories many years ago and encouraged me to write my first book. A talented writer, playwright and actress, Jan is the friend I like beside me when we are launching a book. She can bring out the essence of the book, both the funny and the tragic sides.

To my long-suffering readers – Anna Yang, Di Godbier and Tom Richardson. Thank you for reading, listening and your comments. You proved that the book was readable as well as funny in many parts, heartbreaking in others. Di, your insights through your brother's war experiences and your own travel, made parts of my book more alive to me.

Thank you to my family, my brothers Garry and Ian, who encouraged me throughout and understood that the reliving of dad's life was not always easy. Thank you Danielle, Kate and Brian, my children who put up with my constant repetition of so much that I was writing.

Lyn McGettigan is the eldest of Jack and Pearl's three children. She was raised in the country and the city.

After leaving St Ursula's College Kingsgrove, she graduated from Bathurst Teachers' College in 1965. Lyn married a publican in 1971 and obtained her Hospitality qualifications at Ryde TAFE and from Cornell University. In 2001 she graduated from the University of New England with a BA in Archaeology (Aboriginal) and Palaeoanthropology. She has taught, trained and examined in Hospitality, and worked with Indigenous people.

Lyn has published **Behind the Bar Room Door**, a humorous memoir of her life as a publican's wife, articles for newspapers, for anthologies and for social media. She intends to keep writing.

Order from The Mosh Shop
www.themoshshop.com.au/products/behind-the-bar-room-door-by-lyn-mcgettigan

Order from Angus and Robertson
www.angusrobertson.com.au/behind-bar-room-door-lyn-mcgettigan/p9781925959475